A Leap of  Faith

Alcyon Ruth Fleck

ʀ

REVIEW AND HERALD® PUBLISHING ASSOCIATION
HAGERSTOWN, MD 21740

The author assumes full responsibility for the accuracy
of all facts and quotations as cited in this book.

This book was
Edited by Gerald Wheeler
Designed by Pierce Creative/Matthew Pierce
Cover illustration by Marcus Mashburn
Typeset: 11/15 Palatino

PRINTED IN U.S.A.

07 06 05 04 03   5 4 3 2 1

R&H Cataloging Service
Fleck, Alcyon Ruth, 1921-
        Leap of faith.

        1. International Children's Care.   2. Orphanages—Guatemala.
I. Title.

362.732

ISBN 0-8280-1757-3

A Leap of Faith

Other books by this author:
    Child of the Crossfire

Dedication

One person more than any other deserves the credit for having the vision and the persistence in making International Children's Care a reality. That is Elder Robert Folkenberg. I wondered many times why he kept on my trail for more than a year to accept the responsibility of creating and directing this program. He denies my allegation that he couldn't find anyone else willing to do it!

As I have worked with him through many years on the ICC board, I have recognized his valuable counsel and direction. I have seen his concern and dedication, as well as his love for these abandoned and homeless children. On his frequent visits to the homes, the children's enthusiastic response with hugs and kisses demonstrates that they see him as a person who truly cares about them.

As you read this story, I'm sure you will agree with me that God chose Bob to lead in creating a program for orphaned children. He believes that we, as Adventist Christians, need to demonstrate to the world what God's character is like, and that we can show this by our love and concern for His forgotten little children. With my heartfelt appreciation to Bob for his part in making ICC possible, and his encouragement to me personally in helping with its growth around the world, I gratefully dedicate this book.

Contents

Introduction

During the years I have spent working with International Children's Care, as a founder in 1978, and through December of 2000 as director of children's services, people have asked me again and again, "How did you happen to do this?"

It is a question that cannot be answered in a few words. Some people who already know the story have urged me to write it for others. After pondering the possibility for years, I have finally done so, hoping to encourage others to be willing to follow God's leading in spite of difficulties and feelings of inadequacy. Beyond that, I want to share what I have learned about faith and leaning completely on God and His promises.

As you read the story you will understand that leading such a large project was not my idea, even though I had always dreamed of helping homeless children. Only through a series of dramatic personal experiences could God convince me that creating a program for homeless and abandoned children was His idea. For some reason unknown to me, in spite of my lack of ability and training, He placed this responsibility on my shoulders.

I have to confess that had I foreseen the difficulties, the dangers, and how it would completely consume my life for all these years, I might never have had the courage to begin. But God knew the future, and He gave me the strength, the courage, and the faith to meet every challenge.

Someday I may write the story of how God led in my life, preparing me for this years before. He even directed events in giving me the right husband, one who would support me every inch of the way. Besides being the love of my life, Ken has been my Rock of Gibraltar to pray and work with me through all the problems and challenges.

When we think back to the small, humble beginning of International Children's Care and see what it is today, we ourselves can hardly fathom it. God has blessed this program far beyond anything we could ask or think. Although we started with one home and one child, now we have more than 1,200 children around the world in our care. Somehow, no matter how much we grow, God always provides for His children. With just our newsletter each month as the principle means of fund-raising, we know it is a miracle! We have learned through experience that God can provide the money, but He is often short of people to be His hands and feet down here on earth.

As I write this story, my prayer is that it will inspire many to trust God implicitly, and to know that when He gives us something to do, He also helps us do it.

1 Disaster in Guatemala

"*L*ook at the headlines!" I called to Ken, my husband. "There's been a devastating earthquake in Guatemala. They estimate at least 25,000 victims!"

Guatemala, our first mission field, had been home to us for five years some 25 years before. We knew that earth tremors were common in that volcanic area. Often we had run out to the safety of the street, not knowing how severe each quake would become. But we had never seen real damage. For the next few days we followed the news avidly. When we tried to get through to our mission there, the lines were always jammed. Finally we heard that the damage had been extensive. Besides the dead and missing, thousands of people had lost their homes. What really got my attention was the news that the quake had left at least 5,000 children orphaned and homeless.

Since grade school days I had hoped that someday I could run an orphanage. Our local *Oregon Statesman* newspaper had a serial in the cartoon section called "Little Annie Roonie." I remembered hurrying home each day, finding the paper on the step, and spreading it out to read about what was happening to poor little Annie. She lived in a large orphanage, the kind that depicted all the horrors of the typical orphanages of that day. Miss Meaney, a tall, angular woman, who wielded a heavy hand, made Annie's life a nightmare no matter how hard the girl tried to please. I would go to bed dreaming of the kind of orphanage I would have if I were in charge. *Maybe I can have a place for little orphaned children when I grow up,* I told myself.

One day out of the blue the phone rang, and the director of Adventist Adoption, Lee Anne Bradshaw, was on the line. "Alcyon, I've been investigating the situation in Guatemala involving all the orphans left after the earthquake. I would like to go down and see if there is any way we can provide homes for some of them."

"That would be wonderful!" I answered. "I hope you can do something."

"The problem is that I don't speak Spanish, but I know that you do. If I pay your way, would you be willing to go with me?"

"Well, I will need to talk to Ken, but I would love to go. I have been concerned about conditions there."

After making arrangements, we were on our way. A representative of the Central American Union of Seventh-day Adventists (located in Guatemala City) met us at the airport. The union had made arrangements for us to stay in the Continental Hotel, right in the center of town. With so many news-media people arriving, and so many hotels damaged, it was the only place available. It alarmed us to see that the quake had leveled another small hotel across the street, scattering bricks all over the sidewalk and street. "We have only two usable floors because of damage," the receptionist told us, "the fourth and seventh." We chose the fourth, and then found we had to carry our bags up the stairs. The elevator was not running. Looking down the hall we saw debris from the walls and ceiling still littering the floor. In our room the wall between the bathroom and bedroom had a gaping hole revealing the bathtub. The large windows on the outside wall were so loose that you could see through the cracks around the window casings. We were still standing with our luggage in hand in the middle of the room when we heard another rumble and felt a rocking sensation. "Alcyon, we have to get out of here!" Lee Anne began to cry.

"But, Lee Anne, where will we go? It's night and we can't sleep in the street!" I was frightened too, but a little more used to dangerous situations than she, having been a missionary for years.

We slept what we could—in our clothes—after moving our beds away from the walls. The hotel held together for the few days we were there.

The aftershocks continued, interrupting the church service. People were nervous, but the pastor urged us to have faith and pray for safety.

On Sunday Pastor Robert Folkenberg, the Central American Union secretary and later its president, took us to see some of the devastation. People had set up tents, tarps, or whatever protection they could in the streets. Windows had shattered in those buildings that hadn't collapsed. The authorities had barricaded the roads, but we succeeded in reaching the village west of the city that many believed to be the epicenter of the quake. There we went to a temporary camp set up for victims. Although they had no tents, the people had found pieces of plastic or cardboard and used them to shelter themselves. The camp's inhabitants cooked over open fires. A man, evidently the one appointed to be in charge, met us at the gate. He agreed to take us around to see the victims. "Are there any children left orphaned here?" I asked him.

"Yes, there are. I'll take you to see one little family of six children. The quake killed their father, and an ambulance took the mother away. No one knows what happened to her."

When we found the little group, I saw that the oldest teenage girl was doing her best to care for her siblings. The rest, stair steps in age, were all of them in rags, apparently the same clothes they had worn during the five days since the quake. They had dirty faces, runny noses, and matted hair. The earthquake had left them with nothing. One of the children, a 12-year-old boy, had gone. "He is in the city, looking for our mother," a sister explained. He was going to every hospital or refuge center, asking if his mother was there.

Different groups of charities arrived periodically, bringing rice and beans to the survivors. As I left the camp my heart felt heavy. *What will ever happen to these children?*

During the next few weeks Lee Anne tried every avenue that she could think of in an effort to bring some of the children out for adoption, but it was impossible. No one knew if the children still had family members somewhere. And the government had no legal program set up to let children leave the country.

Pastor Folkenberg, a ham radio operator, took an active role in the government's emergency efforts. He obtained help in setting up a temporary tent village and cooperated with the emergency activities in many ways. I heard that he was in touch with a group of doctors in Loma Linda, California, called La Liga. They pledged to raise money for an orphanage if the Cental American Union would supervise in organizing it.

Some months later Pastor Folkenberg phoned me. "Alcyon, we have money now for a building for orphan children. There is plenty of room out in the Peten area at our mission school. It has a large homestead type property, more than 2,000 acres, with a river running through it. I have arranged with the union and mission to dedicate part of this land for the orphanage project."

"That sounds great!" I answered. "When do you expect to do this?"

"That's what I'm calling you for. I know you have always worked with needy children during your years in the mission field. We are asking you to head this up."

"What do you mean, Bob? I haven't had experience in administration. I've been just a pastor's wife. While I couldn't head it up, I would help out in any way I could," I replied, almost breathless. Actually, I had to remember my dreams from childhood. To be involved in a project like this would be a thrill for me.

When I told Ken about the phone call, he insisted, "Of course you could do it. You have had lots of experience caring for abandoned children in our home through the years. I thought this was your dream—to some day have an orphanage." Then he added realistically, "Naturally it will take some doing."

We had recently returned to the States from Costa Rica, and Ken had taken a pastorate in the Oregon Conference. As we discussed it later, he said, "You know I am close to retirement, though it would mean an early retirement. That might be the biggest problem. You couldn't go alone."

"No, of course I couldn't. And I couldn't do it alone, either. I would need your help."

During the following days we talked about the proposed orphanage almost continually. Robert Folkenberg had phoned again, letting me know that I wasn't off the hook. Ken agreed that he would give me a year of his time, and then he had some other plans of his own for retirement that also involved the mission field. But we still had to deal with the problem of retiring earlier than we had planned.

Once when Bob called, I asked for more details. "Is this to be sponsored by the church? Even though you have $40,000 for the first building, how will the orphanage be financed?"

"Oh, that's easy," he responded. "You just find sponsors for each child."

Now I learned that I would be responsible for locating support for the institution. The church did not have a policy or budget for an orphanage. We were happy to go as volunteers, but how would we feed and care for the children? That thought made us hesitate. If we could develop a plan to make money to support the children, we might accept the assignment, but we knew that any resources we could find would limit us to only a few children. To ask for money from other people was repugnant to us. What if the project failed? We would feel obligated to the people who had supported it.

2 Will We or Won't We?

Before long we received a telephone call from Iver Christensen that began to make us wonder if God was trying to tell us something. Iver and his wife, Jacquie, had recently spent some time with Maranatha rebuilding churches after the earthquake.

"We know that you worked for years in Guatemala," he began. "A group of us who helped after the earthquake are wondering if you might know of a project we could be involved in down there."

"You know, it is strange that you called," I told him. "The fact is that Pastor Folkenberg is asking me to help them start an orphanage in Guatemala."

"Hey! That's something we would really be interested in!" he replied with excitement. "Tell me more about it."

I explained all that I knew. "Ken and I haven't given an answer yet. But I would like to know what your group would think of this, and what the possibilities might be."

"I'll contact some of our friends," he said. "We'll get back to you."

Then one day Jacquie phoned. "Alcyon, we've talked to several people about the idea of an orphanage in Guatemala, and we are all wondering if you and Ken would be willing to meet with us to tell us more about it and answer our questions."

"Of course," I replied. "Even though we haven't made any promises yet, we would like to know what you think."

The number of people who showed up at the meeting surprised us. It had attracted at least 20 business and professional people, all interested in the orphaned children of Guatemala. Some of them we had known slightly, but most were strangers to us. We spent at least two hours talking about what a group like this could accomplish. In addition, we discussed the legal documents that we would need to operate as a nonprofit group to send money overseas. Then we explored organization, policies, and long-range goals. The group included people with many skills. And most important of all, they were dedicated to helping others and had the faith to believe it could be done. At the end they decided that I should go to Guatemala, see the property offered to us, talk to the local union and government officials, and then bring them a report.

The project still had no funding, but Ken said we would stand the expense of my trip. As soon as possible, I made plans to go. Bob met my flight and arranged to take me with some others in the union's plane out to the northern Peten area of Guatemala. It was in an undeveloped jungle region where the mission had recently started a new school.

The school's director, Jim Bechtel, took us around the property. We saw the areas they were not using where we might put an orphanage. Finally we decided on a front corner of 300 acres at the entrance of the mission property. The fact that it was a remote part of Guatemala would have its drawbacks. The road out there from the city was paved only part of the way, and quickly deteriorated during bad weather. It would be a nine- or 10-hour trip by road at best. However, the remoteness could be a blessing, providing a sanctuary for children brought from the hovels and poverty of the country. The air was fresh and clean, the pine forest beautiful, and the property would not cost us anything. We could begin building immediately. The site had no electricity. The only water was the river and the rain, which was plentiful. The mission school would be half a mile or so from us and would offer a support system. I felt positive about the possibilities there for children, but I still hoped they would find another person to head it up. At least I would help.

The Committee, as we called ourselves, met again to hear my report. While impressed, they also realized the seriousness and permanence of the commitment they would be making. We decided to do more research, get more ideas of how we might support an orphanage, and examine the steps needed to make the project a reality.

I still struggled with the doubts I had about my ability and preparation for such a challenge. After all, I didn't have a college degree and was only a pastor's wife, but they assured me that my experience was the most important thing. Also, I hesitated to ask my husband to accept an early retirement. It would mean taking us away from our four children and 10 grandchildren. I had already neglected them a lot during our years in the mission field. Where was my duty?

To find answers I began to study the Bible and the writings of Ellen White. I prayed earnestly. My husband assured me of his support and actually encouraged me to take the step. At one point he asked me, "Exactly what is the reason you are hesitating? I know this has always been your dream."

After thinking a few minutes, I answered, "Well, for one thing, I am realizing what a permanent commitment I would be making. I'm afraid I will get tired and want to quit. After all, I've never done anything that depended so heavily on me before."

"No, my dear. I know you. You will never try to bail out."

We lived close to a forested area with a view of the Columbia River. Usually each morning I walked a path that circled through the woods. I had found a little protected cove in the trees that was my private sanctuary. There I could pray in solitude. One morning, as I listened to the sounds of nature around me, the unsolved problem of the orphanage filled my mind. Nearing my sanctuary, I felt the need to pray. God seemed so near as I tearfully pleaded for His guidance. "Father, I want to do this. I've always wanted to help children. Why do I feel so hesitant? I need Your help. If I accept this responsibility, I must know for sure that it is Your idea, not mine." Suddenly the thought came to me. *Your problem is a fear of failure.*

When I reached home, I pulled down the book I had been reading, *Positive Christian Living*, by E. G. White. As I read, certain statements seemed to stand out as if printed in bold letters. One particularly caught my attention. "But when we give ourselves wholly to God and in our work follow His directions, He makes Himself responsible for its accomplishment. He would not have us conjecture as to the success of our honest endeavors. Not once should we even think of failure. We are to cooperate with One who knows no failure.

"We should not even talk of our own weakness and inability" (p. 330). I sat reading those words again and again. *Is God telling me something?*

But I wasn't ready yet for a decision. I still needed to know for sure. *Is this God's plan? Could He possibly be calling me to do something this big?* That day as I went about my work, my mind was far away. I began to go back a few years to something that had happened when we had lived in Costa Rica. *Could that possibly have a bearing on what I am facing now?*

3 Why Are You Afraid?

*D*uring our stay in Costa Rica I had come down with the flu. It had left me with a hard cough. Then one day I began to hear a strange noise in my right ear—like a bell ringing with every heartbeat. When it continued for several days, I went to an ear specialist to find out if my cold had settled in my ear. After the examination the doctor looked at me seriously and said, "This isn't in your ear; this is a vascular problem. You need to see a specialist."

Ken felt that I should go to the States for tests. We still had a home in Washington that hadn't sold, so I returned alone. From there I called our son, Ron, a medical doctor practicing in Montana. With his counsel, I made an appointment with a neurologist in Portland. The specialist scheduled an angiogram at Portland Adventist Hospital. They performed it through an artery in my neck. When I woke up, the doctor soon came to tell me, "You have a tumor on the jugular vein." He went on to explain that I needed surgery immediately. For someone who had never even had a tonsillectomy, this was devastating news.

I called Ken, then got in touch with Ron, who began researching the problem. In the meantime, I went through a spiritual struggle there in the big empty house by myself. The noise in my head was becoming unbearable. Unable to escape it, I couldn't sleep. My nerves were frazzled. I had been a pastor's wife, a missionary, but now I wondered, *Where is my faith? Is God with me or not?*

In my desperation to find relief I would take hot and cold showers, sometimes several a day. That seemed to relieve my nerves and drown out the noise temporarily. One morning in the shower, as I cried and prayed, something spoke to me. Whether it was an audible voice or not, I don't know. But I heard the words so plainly, "Why are you so afraid? Don't you know you have a Father who loves you?"

Startled, I turned off the water, got out of the shower, and dressed, feeling as if I were anyplace else but there. Heading right to the phone, I called my son. "Ron! Something has happened. I won't have to have that surgery. I think God has spoken to me!" After I told him all about it, I had to acknowledge, though, that the noise was still there.

"Mom, I think God is assuring you that your surgery will be successful. You must go ahead with medical help."

I think it was that same day that I received a call from a close friend, Dr. Lowell Kattenhorn, a surgeon at Portland Adventist Hospital. "Alcyon," he said, "some of us have been looking at your X-rays. We've put them on the staff bulletin board under the classification 'Rare Birds.' What are you planning to do?"

"I don't know yet. The problem is that when we volunteered to take off a couple of years on our own to help the college in Costa Rica, we lost our insurance. I suppose this surgery will cost a lot."

"Listen, Alcyon. I have discussed this with others, and we all agree that it is a vascular problem and that you need a vascular surgeon, not a neurosurgeon. Let me do a little research."

Even though I accepted Ron's opinion that I needed to proceed with medical help, the experience in the shower had made a powerful impression that has not abated to this day. Whatever happened, I now knew that I was assured of God's love and care, and that He knew best. I was ready to trust my life in His hands.

Soon Dr. Kattenhorn called back. "Alcyon, you need to know that this isn't just any surgery," he explained. "You need the best there is. I have called different places, including Loma Linda. Dr. Lewis Smith is head of vascular surgery there. He was my teacher. Not only is he the best I could ever think of, but he is a dedicated Christian. You can have confidence in him. I talked to him and told him your problem. He has done some similar cases. It is called arteriovascular malformation. You have no doubt had it since birth, and it has just now become a problem. But it can be life-threatening and needs to be taken care of. The good news is that Dr. Smith will do this free of charge."

My eyes welled with tears. *God really is taking care of me. I can do whatever I have to do in confidence.* "Thank you so much, Lowell. You can't know how much I appreciate your help."

"I'll put you in touch with Dr. Smith's office," he went on, "so you can make an appointment with him."

I had lots to tell Ron and Ken. Arrangements were made for me to go to Loma Linda for the surgery. I knew they would shave some of my head, so I laughingly told our daughter, Carolyn, "I'll need to buy a wig to wear back!" She planned to be with me for the surgery, and Ken would meet us in Loma Linda.

I can honestly say that I made plans for my surgery with total optimism and faith, just eager to get it over with, to stop the horrible pounding in my head. By now people could put their head against mine and hear it. My prayers were full of thankfulness to God for His interest in me, and His love that He had assured me of.

The first day in Loma Linda involved another angiogram, this time with a catheter through the groin up into my head. It was painful, feeling as if fire was coursing through my head. The doctor explained that they had to keep me awake because of the risks involved. When they shot the pictures, I sensed they were honing in on one area. Then Dr. Smith scheduled the surgery for the next day.

Ken and Carolyn were there with me as they brought the gurney and strapped me on it. But just as the nurses from surgery began to wheel me away, a voice came through on the PA system. "Hold it on Mrs. Fleck. Take her to the doctors' consulting room first." Ken accompanied me as I rode in a wheelchair.

Dr. Smith was there. He had the X-rays of my angiogram on a lighted board. "We have been consulting on your case, Mrs. Fleck, and we feel that we cannot go ahead with surgery. The damage is too widespread and complicated. The risks are too great for you."

Needless to say, my hopes plummeted and my faith suffered a blow. "There is another procedure they are working on that will be less invasive," the doctor went on. "It will be something they can insert into the ruptured area, then guide it with a magnet from the outside, to stop up the hole that is causing the problem. I want to send you for tests of your heart. This is the danger—that the blood coming back through the veins to the heart could cause cardiac arrest. I'm sorry for your disappointment, but I feel I cannot put you through such a risk now."

I had gone to sleep the night before in the hospital, thinking, *This is the last night I'll have to put up with this. I can hardly wait.* Needless to say, I now felt numb, hardly able to believe what Dr. Smith was saying.

The tests done on my heart gave them assurance that, with caution, I could hold off for another year or two. *Another year or two! How could I ever live through this that long?* I have to admit that I was devastated. Then, beginning to pray again, I asked God to reaffirm my faith. Through the next year and a half I went through my Bible, underlining every promise I found, and fastening my faith on God's Word. He had spoken. Now I just needed to trust Him. I could sleep only for two or three hours at a time, and then only when I was extremely tired. But I survived—one day at a time.

4 It's Gone!

A year and a half later a group of American women, most of them volunteers at the college in Costa Rica, wanted to start a prayer group. One of them had brought several of Glenn Coon's books on the ABCs of prayer. They wanted me to lead the prayer group. Only one of them knew of my problem. We decided to each bring one request to the group, and we would all pray about it at the same time of day. I did not mention my health problem. Instead, I asked for prayer for my daughter, who was going through serious problems in her marriage. She hadn't been in touch with us as much as usual. Perhaps she wasn't ready for our advice. My concern for her and her family overshadowed my problems with my health.

By now we had been meeting for two weeks. I had been reading one of Coon's books, *Path to the Heart,* and focusing on the promises I was finding in God's word. It was Mother's Day. Although we didn't have a phone in our house, I prayed earnestly that morning, "Lord, would I be asking too much for a sign—a sign just to let me know You are hearing me and answering my prayer?

Carolyn hasn't called for quite a while, but if You are taking care of this, please have her phone today."

Early afternoon someone called me to the phone. It was Carolyn. "Mom, I just want to wish you a happy Mother's Day and to tell you how much I love you." That was all. We didn't discuss her problem. But I went back to the house, weeping, and praising God. *Oh, thank You, Lord, for giving me that assurance! I know I can trust You and not worry anymore about this problem. You love her even more than I do.* For the rest of the day my heart was light. Even though the noise in my head was still there, I didn't pay much attention to it.

That night I told my husband about my prayer and our daughter's phone call. We thanked the Lord together. Then Ken reminded me, "By the way, remember the letter from Dr. Smith? He wants to see you as soon as possible and thinks they may be ready to help you. Since we are going to Canada for Rick and Sharon's wedding soon, you need to write him and make an appointment."

Although I did sit down and write him, I was so elated over the phone call that I didn't give the potential surgery a lot of thought. As I went to bed I kept thanking God again and again for hearing my prayers. Our bed was right by an open window.

When I awoke, I was startled to see that it was daylight. Somehow I had slept all night, the first time since my vascular problem had started. The birds were singing outside my window. Thinking I was dreaming, I rubbed my face, trying to wake up. It was so quiet. Then Ken reached over and asked, "What's the matter?"

"I don't know. It's so quiet. And I can't hear my head pounding."

Alarmed, he raised up in bed. He knew there was danger of the blood bursting through the damaged vessel, something that could mean instant death. "Are you all right?"

"Yes, but I can't hear anything. It is so quiet."

He put his head down on mine and listened. "I don't hear anything either. Are you sure you are all right?"

"Yes, I feel fine, but the noise is gone."

Ken looked at me intently, and then, propping himself up on his elbow, nearly shouted, "I think you have been healed! Praise God!"

We stayed there talking for a while. I was almost afraid to move for fear the clanging would start again. All during that day my husband would watch me carefully. "Are you still OK? Are you sure?"

"I feel great," I would answer. All that day I went about my work with a thrill that I can't describe. The sense of God's unfathomable love to me filled me with awe. "The realization that, somehow, God reached down and touched me through the night was almost more powerful than to know I was healed," I later told Ken.

Although we did not have the evidence at that time, my confidence that God had heard my prayer for my daughter's marriage was also rewarded a short while later.

Later that day I added a PS to my letter to Dr. Smith, telling him briefly that the noise had stopped and that I would call him when we came through Loma Linda.

It was a Friday when I phoned him. "Where are

you?" he asked when he answered. "I want to see you."
Then he made an appointment to meet me in his office
Saturday night. After examining me carefully, he just
stood back and looked at me. "It just isn't there. I can't
explain it. Something very unusual has happened."

"Dr. Smith, can a problem like this go away on its
own?" my husband asked.

"Well," he answered, "if a river can stop in its tracks.
It's the same thing. Just give credit where credit is due!"

As we drove away from the hospital, I rode along
deep in thought, then remarked, "Remember the experience I told you about when I was home alone—how
God spoke to me? I'll never forget the words: 'Why are
you so afraid? Don't you know you have a Father who
loves you?'"

"No, my dearest. We must never forget what God
has done. It is a miracle!"

5 The Decision

*A*ll day I thought about the phone call from Guatemala and the challenge it had thrust into my life. Reviewing the amazing event of almost five years before, I had to wonder, *Could God have had this in mind all along? Was He preparing me for something special—even for this?* Finally I came to a decision. *If I can be sure that God is sending me this call, then I have no choice but to accept. I wouldn't want to try something that big without knowing that He is behind it.*

More and more I found myself leaning toward telling Bob Folkenberg that I would do my best. But first I needed to talk to him again and to make sure the Committee was ready to move ahead. Ken assured me that he believed the request was from God and that he personally would support me—at least for a year! He was 62 and still had to work out his early retirement, but he felt that could be done.

At the Oregon camp meeting I met Bob Folkenberg. He drew me apart from the pavilion. "I need to talk to you," he explained. We walked over to a quiet place under a tree. Then he began. "Are you going to do this?"

"Well, first of all, we have never discussed what kind of an orphanage you have in mind," I replied.

"I suppose we'll just build a dormitory over there on that land near the mission school."

"I'm not interested in that kind of an orphanage," I told him. I had long dreamed of a village concept that placed the children in individual homes with Christian houseparents, thus creating a family-like structure.

"Well, what kind of an orphanage are you interested in?" he questioned.

"If you have time, I'll explain."

He smiled. "I have plenty of time. Go ahead."

I described what I thought was the ideal situation for children who had suffered the loss of parents. "They need to feel they are part of a family. In fact, Mrs. White states that any institution for orphaned children should be based on the plan of a family—a Christian family."

When I finished he said, "That's exciting! Let's do it!"

Returning home, I sat down to outline a proposal for a village plan for orphaned children. It was quite detailed. When the Committee met, I presented it, and they, too, were excited. We voted to go ahead, providing all the pieces came together, especially the legal requirements. In the meantime, I would go back to Guatemala with the idea of making more detailed plans, including the site of the first home. But I still had not made a commitment to Bob.

While we were arranging my trip, Ken suggested, "You know there's one more thing you should do before signing your life away. It's been five years since God healed you, but I think you should see Dr. Smith one more time. Explain the project and the long-term commitment it involves. We need to be sure you won't be getting into something that will demand too much of you."

When I walked into Dr. Smith's office, he had some other specialists there. He also had my complete file before him. They were all going to examine me and confer. When they finished, Dr. Smith turned to me and said, "I would give anything to get into your head and know what happened, but you are fine."

I explained the type of commitment I was making. "You know that I can't send orphans back where they came from so I just want to be sure that I have no limitations."

He put his hand on my shoulder and smiled. "You should go and do anything you want, and God bless you!"

I walked out of his office, again amazed at what had happened in my life. *Was Dr. Smith's report the sign I needed to be sure this was from God?* As I entered the waiting room, to my surprise I saw Bob Folkenberg sitting there. "Bob, what are you doing here? You're supposed to be in Guatemala."

"I'm looking for you, Alcyon. I need an answer. Are you going to do it or not?"

"What if I don't do it?" I asked.

"Then we will send the money back."

"Do you mean that there will be no orphanage if I don't do it?"

"Exactly!" he answered, looking at me intently.

Glancing down and with a prayer in my heart, I hesitated. Then I looked at him again. "I guess I have no other choice. Yes. Count on me. With God's help I'll do my best."

I went on to Guatemala with mixed feelings. Although all the events that had transpired to propel me into this new venture left me in awe, at the same time I knew that the experience would try my faith to the limit. But it also would bring thrills and satisfaction beyond my wildest imagination. I knew I had lots to learn and realized that I didn't have the preparation or wisdom in myself. But, trusting God implicitly, Ken and I would take one day at a time and see what He would do.

All during that trip I had my notebook handy. I began to lay plans on how we should start, the staff we would need, the amount of money we would require for the first year of operation. When I stood on the ground where we decided to build the first cottage, I felt both thrilled and a little frightened. But I could hardly wait to see a house there full of children.

Flying back to the United States gave me ample time for reflection. Some moments I almost panicked. The challenge was so huge. And still another problem lurked in the back of my mind. I remembered those children at the camp we had visited. They were anything but attractive, almost repulsive. *The ones we take in are going to be like that. Do I have enough love in my heart for such children?* I realized that I didn't, and that I couldn't do a good job without it. *Lord, it will take the kind of love You have for people like me for us to help these children,* I began to pray. *Please give me that kind of love.*

When I met with the Committee again we were ready for serious business. They all stood solidly behind me, and we proceeded to draw up the plans for beginning the project. We enlisted our son-in-law, John Stewart, an attorney, to help us with the legal documents, which he did free of charge. Then we drew up a list of all the people we could think of for the first monthly newsletter that has become a tradition now for nearly a quarter century. The initial list of 50 people grew rapidly. At that same meeting we also discussed a name for our new organization. Finally we came up with International Children's Care, Inc. We didn't know how far it would go, but we wanted to provide for whatever growth the Lord would permit. Donations began to come in. Jacquie agreed to be our volunteer secretary, and our first office was in her back bedroom. She continued to give us valuable help for a number of years.

Ken and I knew we would have to spend a lot of time in Guatemala. But we also needed to be at the home office to help with the fund-raising. So finding a house sitter, we went to Guatemala in December of 1978. There we rented a house in the capital that had room to take in children while we prepared the first cottage out in the jungle.

During our visit to Guatemala I contacted some old friends, Maria and Luis Feldmann. Maria agreed to volunteer some time. We sat together in their living room and discussed a name for the new children's village out in the Peten. Since pine trees filled our property, we all agreed on Adventist Country Home, The Pines (Los Pinos).

When Ken and I moved into that first rented house in the city and prepared it to receive children, we knew that International Children's Care was launched.

6 Our First Baby

"Marla! What do you have there?" I asked one of the volunteers at the mission school.

"It's a baby! It's a baby girl, but she is terribly sick," the woman answered.

"But where did you get her?" I questioned.

"Well, I went out to a village with the Bechtels and some of the other Maranatha workers. They were conducting a free clinic. A woman came up with this little girl in her arms. She said that her baby was dying, and that she was desperate! I think that since we are Americans, she thought we could help her."

"Here, let me see her. Did they tell you how old she is?"

"Yes, she is 10 months old."

As I began to examine the baby I noted the dull, lifeless expression in her eyes and the pallid color of her skin. The child was swollen and puffy with edema. "My! Just look at her ankles," I observed. "They are so swollen they are cracked and bleeding." Examining her further I found infected sores all over her body. "But how did you expect to take care of a sick baby in your room in the girl's dormitory?"

"I guess I didn't think it all out, but some of the other women said they would help me if I took her. I just couldn't say no. Did I do the wrong thing? We thought that she could be your first orphan."

"But she isn't an orphan. Didn't you say that she has a mother?" I asked, still staring at the pitiful little bundle.

"Yes, her mother gave her to us so that we could help her get well. I guess she has a father too, at least there was a man and some more children with her," Marla explained. "I couldn't understand her, of course, but Mrs. Bechtel said that this family had already lost five children with dysentery. I think they were frantic to do anything to save this one. We couldn't refuse to help her, could we?"

"No, of course you couldn't, Marla. I'm just concerned about the responsibility you have taken on. What if the baby should die? We haven't begun taking in children yet, especially such a sick baby as this one." Then studying the child thoughtfully, I added, "I'll see what we can do. First of all, we need to get this baby to a doctor. If you and the other women can care for her in the dormitory for a few days, it will give us time to get her some medical help at least."

Vonnie Bechtel helped me take the baby to the nearby army hospital. The commander of the military base that adjoined the mission property had been friendly to the mission school. He often allowed the Bechtels to take advantage of the army medical facilities. "The army has the best doctors available in this area," Vonnie told me.

The doctor was willing to help us. It didn't take him long to recognize the symptoms of dysentery, malnutrition, and dehydration. Nearly every family in that primitive area had lost children from those killer diseases. "The baby is very sick," he told us, "but if you get the prescriptions that I give you and provide her constant care, I think she will recover."

On the way back along the narrow jungle road Vonnie and I discussed the baby's possible future. "We really came to furnish homes for orphaned children," I said, "and we aren't equipped to be a hospital, but I agree that this baby needs help. Are the parents going to want her back?"

"I don't know that, but I do know that this family is desperately poor. The mother is pregnant again, and the father is sick with asthma and can't work. I doubt they can ever give this baby what she needs."

"Well, let's see if there is any way we can take care of her until she is well," I said. "Then we'll observe what happens."

Our first cottage was not yet ready for occupancy, and we still had not hired a director. So we certainly were not ready to receive children—and yet we had come to rescue them. This little girl might die if we didn't take her. Had God really brought us our first infant?

I discussed it with Ken and then with the Bechtels. Jim Bechtel came up with an idea. "You know, there's an empty house down by the river that some volunteers, the Rarys, built for themselves, and then they couldn't stay. It might be remodeled for you to start in until the first cottage is finished."

"Let's go down and see it," I quickly suggested. I really did want to find a way to keep this little girl until she was well, and that could be several weeks or longer."

The little cottage was rustic, to say the least, but it had three bedrooms, a bathroom with plumbing that didn't work, a small living area, and an adjoining building that housed the kitchen and eating area. We looked it over carefully. I could see that with some effort it could serve as a temporary house. It was close to the river. Fortunately, the trucks of material that volunteers had sent to the mission school had some furniture and other supplies we could use. Jim assured me that some of the older students could help with labor. Now, the remaining problem was, "Who can we use as an interim director, or at least someone to care for this one baby?"

That evening we discussed the situation with the volunteers who had offered to assist Marla. "We will help while we are here," they said. Then, one continued, "Marla is a very responsible young lady and she is so taken with the baby. I don't think she has a job right now. Maybe she would be willing to stay on for a few weeks and aid you."

That might work, I thought to myself. *If Vonnie Bechtel would be willing to help her. When I am here, I can do it. I will need to be here quite a bit in the next couple months, anyway, getting the first cottage ready.*

Marla was more than willing to stay. For her this was a volunteer's dream—to care for a little baby like Anna (which they had begun calling her). The next two or three days we spent feverishly remodeling the Rary house. Marla, with help from her friends, cared for

Anna, giving her the medicines to free her of the parasites that were eating her life away. It was a little traumatic for Marla to discover white round worms in the child's diaper, but she wasn't daunted. "Poor little baby!" she would croon as she cuddled and loved her new charge.

By the time the Maranatha group left for home, we had the Rary house ready. As Ken and I surveyed the results I was amazed at how homey it was. "You know it really looks like a home. We'll take this room here for ours for now, and we will make this our home for a little while."

"Well, my dear," he said, "I have never seen it to fail. No matter what kind of a place we have to live in, even a prune shed like we used in one of our first districts, you manage to make it a real home."

"That's my domestic juices rising to the occasion," I laughed. "The truth of it is, I love to take something like this little shack and turn it into a home. And to make it into a shelter for children is just frosting on the cake."

We still had the rented house in the city to think about. Since The Pines was out in the jungle, we needed a center where services were available for buying materials, for banking, and for legal services. We found a girl to help us with the housework and to take care of things when we were gone. As soon as we could find a qualified woman to take care of children, we would accept babies there, too.

It was somewhat of a challenge to bounce back and forth from Los Pinos, our city center, and Battle

Ground, Washington. We still had to spearhead the fund-raising in the United States and consult with the committee that we now called the International Children's Care board. Ken and I found that we had to split up and travel separately in order to cover all our bases. Besides the need for supervision at each place, we had the problem of expenses. ICC began on a shoestring. But we were beginning to learn that God was with us. At every step we sensed His providence. For the first year of operation we had budgeted $20,000. That would provide for growth toward our goal of 10 homes at Poptun as well as provide food and care for the children. Afterwards we realized that we had been a little naive. We couldn't possibly anticipate all of our needs.

After we installed Anna—our very first baby—and her caretaker, Marla, in the Rary house, Marla exclaimed, "This is so neat! I can wash clothes in the river, just like the Indian women do! And I can go swimming every day!"

The Machaquila River is truly a beautiful body of water as it winds through the jungle. Except after heavy rains, the water is clear and almost bathwater temperature. Right below the Rary house there is a swimming hole with boulders to climb on around it. The jungle trees hang over the river on both sides, and wild parrots chatter through the trees. "Do you realize we have our own swimming hole for the children? They can learn to swim here!" I told Ken late one afternoon as we sat on the rocks by the river.

"Well, my dear," he commented, "I guess you can

say that you are finally realizing your dream. One house is almost finished, we have a temporary cabin here right by a beautiful river, and we have our very first baby!"

"I can hardly believe it," I sighed.

7 Missing Over the Jungle

After a hot and busy day, Ken and I decided to cool off in the river. The shadows were falling, and only the sound of the rapids above us, mixed with the various jungle noises, broke the silence.

"What a paradise!" my husband exclaimed as we climbed up on a rock. "It's as if we are in a different world!"

"I know," I mused. Then as an afterthought I added, "Only I wonder if this might be the time of day when animals come to drink. Do you suppose there are dangerous wild animals close by?"

"Well, I wouldn't be surprised. They say there are jaguars, panthers, tapirs, and different kinds of monkeys on the other side of the river."

I kept my eye over there, where the jungle crowded down to the water. At one spot I noticed an opening in the foliage and asked, "Could that be the animal path?"

He laughed. "You would think of that!"

After our evening meal, Ken went to the school to talk to Jim Bechtel. When he returned he announced,

"Lindy is flying the plane to Guatemala City tomorrow morning. He and Jim are taking an American couple in to catch their plane. They said there is room for me."

The Bechtels' son, Lindy, a pilot, was helping his parents and he had brought a plane to Guatemala.

"I thought we were going on the army plane on Tuesday," I objected. General Lucas, the commander of the army base, lets us ride in the military aircraft when it has room.

"I know, but I was thinking I would have an extra day in town if I went tomorrow. You could come on Tuesday as planned."

The next morning I drove Ken, in the old Datsun pickup we had purchased, to the landing strip on the mission property. "Usually I don't take off from this runway because it is short," Lindy commented, "but since none of us have baggage, I think it will be safe."

I waited to watch them leave. As they lifted into the air I noticed, with some concern, that they seemed to be barely skimming the tops of the trees, but they were soon out of sight. Since I needed to arrange for my flight on the military plane on Tuesday I went back to the cabin to get ready. Taking one of our workers, I drove into the village to the army headquarters. As we stopped at the check station I told the soldier, "We need to see General Lucas."

"He isn't here because a little plane went down," the man explained. "He went out to Las Lajas" (the local name for the mission property).

The blood rushed to my head. "Where did it go down?"

"At the runway," he responded.

The Guatemalan army had the only major runway in the area. Hurriedly backing the truck around, I headed that way, ignoring the ruts in the road. Arriving at the gate, I asked the guard, "Did a plane go down?"

"Not as far as I know," he answered.

"I have to find out about this!" I said, returning to the base.

There I met Vonnie Bechtel and Barbara, Lindy's wife. They were going to the army hospital.

"Have you heard that a plane went down?" I asked them.

"No!" they chorused. "Who told you?"

I repeated what the military base guard had told me. Barbara knew what to do. "We need to go to the airport and find out about their flight plan to see if anyone has heard from them. Lindy wouldn't take off without a flight plan. He planned to radio the control tower as he flew over."

But the trip back to the airport was fruitless. They had not heard from her husband.

Walking back toward our two cars, Barbara's face was grave. "Lindy wouldn't go without a flight plan. I can't understand this."

They had taken off at 7:30 a.m. from the small landing strip at The Pines, and it was now after 11:00 a.m. Since the flight takes only an hour, they had had plenty of time to arrive. I suggested that we call our house in the city and talk to Jovita, the maid. I knew that Ken would go there immediately when he arrived.

When she answered, I said, "Jovita, has Pastor Fleck arrived?"

"No, señora. We haven't heard anything from him."

Hanging up the phone, I turned to the others. "He isn't there! What shall we do?"

"I think I'll call the tower in Guatemala City," Barbara decided.

Standing near her as she made the phone call, I noticed her skirt shaking, and I knew I was also trembling all over. Then I realized that Barbara was talking to someone. Apparently she had leaned some news!

When she hung up she turned to us, obviously relieved. "They just had a message from them! They had to set down twice at little airports because of bad weather. First they landed in Coban, but when they took off from there, they had to set down at Rabinal. They have just now taken off again for the city."

With tears of relief we discussed the situation, still not sure that they were out of danger. "You know," I began, "I have often wondered how I would react if someone I love were on a missing plane. I got a taste of that today."

"Me too," Barbara chimed in.

"I can't understand it," Vonnie commented. "That message from the guard is a mystery. He couldn't have known about their problem."

"But why should that guard have given us false information?" I added. "Could it be that they really needed our prayers?" We all agreed that we had been doing exactly that.

Another call to the tower in the city assured us that they had arrived safely.

On the way back through the jungle I kept thinking,

In this program for children we will face many dangers. Just flying back and forth in these old military planes over the dense unpopulated jungle is a risk. But I must learn that I can safely trust in God's providence and protection, no matter what. After all, didn't God tell me, "Why are you afraid? Don't you know you have a Father who loves you?"

In the years that followed we had many reasons to know how faithful our heavenly Father really is.

8 A Hard Decision

*A*nna had improved dramatically. It was time to take her back to her parents, and Marla was ready to return home. One Sabbath afternoon, with the little girl in the prettiest dress that we could find, Ken, Marla, and I drove to the child's home village. Sad and disturbing thoughts filled our minds. We had all become attached to the little charmer. Marla broke the silence. "Is there any chance they will let us keep her?"

"Maybe, a slight chance," I answered, "but I wouldn't count on it. Guatemalan families take a lot of stock in their children."

"But what if she gets sick again and dies?" Marla was almost in tears.

"You know, Marla, Jesus loves her even more than we do," Ken advised. "We'll have to trust Him to take care of this."

Nearing the village I took out the directions that Vonnie had given me. As we drove down a dirt lane between thatched huts we saw a group of children.

"That looks like the other children from Anna's family," Marla observed, "especially the older girl."

It was quickly obvious that the girl was Anna's sister as she ran along beside the car. Soon she disappeared down a pathway, and we knew she had gone ahead to announce our arrival. By the time we climbed out of the pickup, a group of people had congregated around us.

A very pregnant woman made herself known as Anna's mother. Her face was beaming. A tall, thin, middle-aged man stood nearby, obviously the father. The group of people included an old toothless grandmother along with brothers, sisters, and cousins. It was a real welcoming party.

When we handed the baby to her mother, she exclaimed, "I would hardly know her! She is a different baby. Before, she was dying. Oh, how beautiful she is!"

The father courteously invited us to their home, leading the way down the path. Even though it was humble and primitive, the smooth dirt floor was swept clean. With only the grass roof and bamboo walls for a shelter, the chickens, dogs, and pigs had free rein. A lean-to on the back served as their kitchen with nothing more than an open hearth built of mud bricks. We didn't see evidence of any food. "People in this culture provide for only one meal at a time," I explained to Marla. They had stored a stack of ears of dried corn, a staple in their diet, on a makeshift shelf in one of the trees.

As we talked to the couple in Spanish, we learned that the father's health was too poor for him to work. The family was a picture of abject poverty. They explained that when the baby took sick they had had no money for bus fare to go to a doctor or for medicines.

Except for their folk remedies they had no resources.

Still looking into the face of her baby, the mother said sadly, "She has been delicate all her life. Five of our other babies have died, and we thought that she was going to die too. We can never thank you enough."

I knew that reality must be faced. "We have brought your baby back," I began. "She is much better, but she still needs very good care and a special diet." I went on to describe the various formulas, diet, and vitamins we were using.

"I don't think you understand, señora," the father interrupted. "I don't have the money to buy the first can of milk. We are poor people."

"Anna will soon be sick again if she doesn't get good food and care," I explained as gently as possible.

As fate or providence would have it, just at that moment the old diarrhea showed its ugly head. Marla hurried to clean the baby up. Consternation filled the faces of the parents. That symptom was something they greatly feared. "Her delicate system is still very easily upset," I explained. "Apparently she needs more of her medicine." It was obvious that the parents did not want us to leave the infant with them.

As much as I dreaded to do it, I knew that I must try to help them face the situation. "We'll take the baby back, but you will have to make a decision about her. If you feel that you are not able to give her the care that she needs, we will be willing to keep her. That is a hard decision, and you should think it over very carefully."

"We knew a mother who gave her baby up for adoption," the father said. "That would be hard for us to do, but it would be better than to see her in the grave. If we did that, would we ever see her again or hear from her?"

"If she were adopted by a family who is looking for a baby, you might not see her again, but when she is older, she would be free to visit you."

"Would she know who her real parents are?" he asked

"Yes," I answered. "When she is grown, she would know all about you. If you wrote a letter to her, telling why you gave her up, it would be given to her when she is grown."

The mother's eyes were brimming with tears, and the father had bowed his head as he contemplated the dilemma. The grandmother had been listening intently, but now she spoke. "Don't be selfish!" she told the parents. "Think of the opportunity for your child. She will never be hungry again. When she is sick, she will be cared for. You know she is too frail to live like we do. Don't be foolish!"

The father soon raised his head and said to us, "We thank you for what you have already done. Our baby would now be in the ground if you hadn't taken her. She really belongs to you, but this is a very hard decision. May we think about it for a few days? Will you take her back and keep her for us until we can decide?"

We all found it hard to keep our composure. They seemed like good, honest people with deep feelings like everyone else, but their situation in life was so impossible.

If there were just some way to help them keep her, I kept thinking. *But no, it wouldn't work. She would never survive in this environment. Our first thought has to be for her. How can I ever live with such cruel and heart-rending decisions? I am going to have to come to terms with the reality of life here if am going to survive scenes like this.* "Of course we will take her back," I told them, "but we want you to think through your decision very carefully. We will come back next week. Remember, she is your baby, and we will abide by whatever you decide."

As we drove back down the lane, our hearts felt heavy. "How sad for parents to have to make that kind of a decision!" Ken remarked.

"I guess it is wrong of me," Marla said, "but I was praying all the time that we wouldn't have to leave her there. I just couldn't bear to think of it!" And she gave the baby a big hug.

9 May She Stay?

One evening as I walked up the path to the cabin I was thinking, *What a day! That warehouse was like an oven. But it is cool and quiet down here by the river. I wish someone else were running the program so I could just live here and help out!* Then, jerking out of my mood, I told myself, *What's wrong with me? Guess I'm just tired.* Then breathing a prayer, I said aloud, "Lord, at times like this my courage isn't too good. This is such a big undertaking—too big for me—but You have promised never to leave me or forsake me. Please increase my faith and my courage."

Marla met me at the door with Anna in her arms. "How are things going," I asked, "and how's our baby?"

"She is getting better every day. The swelling is almost gone, and she really has an appetite!"

"Good! She has some catching up to do. I see her hair is growing back." Anna's hair had all fallen out when she had been so sick. "By the way, has anyone come down to fix the pump yet?"

"No, I'm still carrying water from the river, but

there is plenty in the rain barrel for drinking. I did a washing in the river today."

"How did you do it? Where was Anna?"

With a glint in her eye, the young woman replied, "I tied her on my back and washed the clothes on a rock down at the river, like all the other women around here do! When I got through, she and I both had a bath."

Laughing, I told her, "It isn't taking you long to turn native, is it!"

Changing the subject, Marla asked, "Do you think that Anna's parents are going to give her to us when we return next Sabbath afternoon?"

"It's hard to say, but we will pray that they will make the right decision."

"What if they give her to us? Will she be adopted?" Marla persisted.

"A family in the United States asked me to find them a little girl. I haven't said anything to them about this baby yet, but if her parents decide to let her be adopted, we'll contact that family."

"What about letting her stay here in one of the homes for children?"

"That's a possibility too, but she is just a baby. It would be better if she could have a real family, and her parents seemed to have that in mind. Another thing, we're just starting and don't even have a permanent director here. There will be other children needing homes. We aren't really ready to care for a little one like this, especially since you will be leaving soon."

Later I heard Ken bounding down the path, ready

for a swim. "I was hoping we would have time for a dip before dark," he shouted.

After a few laps, we stood in water up to our arms, discussing the day's events.

"How is the house coming?" I asked. "Did they get a lot done today?"

"Yes, the tile on the floor is almost finished. Then we need to install the cabinets sent out from town. The carpenter we hired is making the bunk beds and table. It should come together in another week."

"That would work out just right," I told him. "That new woman we are trying out for director should be here by then, and she can live in with the first group of children. I have that family from South America who are volunteering. I'm thinking that we can let them take care of a group of children in this house. Already we've heard about several children in this area who are homeless."

"Then where will we stay?" he questioned.

"Remember we talked about bringing our camper out here from the city. I thought it would serve for now." We had driven it down from the States.

"Well, maybe, if the rains stop and the roads improve."

Marla had supper ready, a fresh fruit salad with bananas, pineapple, cantaloupe, and mangoes that she served with avocado sandwiches. "This is a meal fit for a king!" Ken exclaimed.

After the meal the three of us still sat around the table, talking, as the candlelight threw our faces into a shadow.

"Are we planning to take Anna to her parents tomorrow?" Marla asked.

"Yes," I answered. "I'm sure the family will be watching for us."

Ken and I agreed that we would leave as soon as possible after dinner the next day.

When we drove into the lane the same children were waiting. Soon the rest of the family appeared and once more escorted us to their humble hut.

After exchanging greetings, the father began, "We have discussed our problem with our families and some of our friends. Some think it is a disgrace ever to give one of your children away. But our closest friends understand our situation. If I had good health and could work all the time, it would be a different story. As hard as it will be, we have decided that you should keep our little girl and arrange the best home you can find for her. We have faith in you."

Marla caught her breath, and I was speechless for a moment. "You have made a good decision," I replied, "but we know that it has been a very difficult and painful one. To think only of her welfare demonstrates your real love for her." We arranged to come back the following Monday to take them to the nearest village with a judge to sign papers.

When we returned, Ken explained that the father would have to ride in back, but the mother insisted, "I'll ride back there with him." The two crawled up into the Datsun truck bed and sat on two chairs with their backs to the cab.

Riding into town, I shared my feelings with Ken. "Somehow, it seems all wrong for a mother and father to sit in the back of a truck just to go and sign their baby away. It seems like the last blow to their self-respect."

"I know," he replied. "I feel the same. I suppose they don't look at it as we do. How many times do they even ride instead of walk?"

"I suppose they're thinking of the five little children out in the cemetery. I'm thankful we didn't have to leave Anna there."

When we took them back home, the father said, as he bid us goodbye, "I asked a friend of mine who knows how to read and write to help me with the letter. It is for our little girl when she is old enough to wonder why her parents gave her away. Please save it and be sure she gets it. I would never want her to think that we didn't love her." Then he handed us a folded piece of paper.

As we left I opened the letter. Translated, it said something like this:

"Our dear daughter:

"It is with a great deal of sorrow that your mother and I have agreed to give you to new parents who will raise you. You were gravely ill, and we are very poor. We feared that you were dying and, in desperation, we looked for someone to help us. These bighearted people took you, helped you to get well, and did the things for you that we couldn't. It is only because we did not have the money to buy the food and medicines that you needed that we have given you up. We hope that you will understand and know that we will always love you.

"Your mother and father."

I sat looking at the soiled piece of paper with tears running down my cheeks. "These poor people! That is real love! They may be uneducated, humble, and even ignorant, but I have a lot of respect for them. I will be sure that this little girl finds the best home possible, and that she learns someday about her birth parents who loved her enough to give her away so that she might live!"

10 Please Take Us!

*A*t the end of a long hot day we bounced into The Pines with our camper. It had taken us 12 hours driving from Guatemala City toward the Caribbean coast, then on unpaved, horrible roads into the northern undeveloped jungle. The pickup had no air conditioning except the open windows. I was learning what the word "tropics" really meant. With the dust and bad road that forced us to go slow we both agreed that riding in the old World War II military planes was certainly the way to go.

"That was some trip!" I remarked, climbing out of the pickup in front of the one house that was now finished and buzzing with children. "But at least we're here!"

"We can thank the Lord for that," Ken replied reverently. "Some of those ruts we went through could have wrecked something."

"Probably if someone else had been driving, they might have. You really maneuvered that horrible road like a pro."

Soon children came running to us from the house. It was already dark, and they had just finished eating.

The new director was right behind them. *"¡Que bueno que han llegado!* ["How good that you have arrived!"],"* she exclaimed.

After asking about everything in general, we were eager to hear about the new house parents for the river cabin.

"Oh, yes, they are here, and we already have some children there with them!"

"Good! And I see that you have some children here, too."

"Yes, people are learning about The Pines. Almost everyday I hear about more children that need homes."

The next few days we spent checking on the construction, learning to know the new children, and helping the director organize her program. Marla had moved to the new house with Anna. "How is she doing?" I asked her.

"Better every day and growing. I'm dreading the day I have to leave her. By the way, if you think it is all right, I should probably plan to leave in a week or so."

"Although we'll miss you, I think we'll make it now. We'll move Anna to the city. I have a good woman there helping me with the children. Since Anna will no doubt have an adoptive home before long, it will be better to keep her there."

The construction was progressing on the administration building. It would provide an apartment for the director, a warehouse, and another large room to use for a temporary school. The crews would finish the warehouse first to provide space for the truckloads of supplies that Dave Bechtel, Jim's brother was bringing us with his long-haul trucks.

One morning the director knocked on our camper door. When I opened it, she blurted, "I just heard about a family of eight children whose mother was killed recently. Would you go with me to visit them?"

"Of course. Let's see if Ken wants to accompany us. We'll take the Datsun." Within the hour we were on our way.

As we traveled through the seven miles of jungle to the village of Poptun the director said, "I've been told that the mother was the one who earned the living by cooking food and selling it from her little cart to the passengers on the busses as they came through town. The father had a serious drinking problem.

"One night as she and the two older children—a boy, 15, and a girl, 13—were pulling the cart across the road at the main intersection, a truck came careening around the corner. The driver had been drinking. The boy, seeing the truck bearing down on them, tried to help his mother pull the cart off the road, but he barely escaped himself. The girl ran to the side of the road, but the truck knocked the mother down, and one of the big wheels rolled over her body. In his dazed condition—when he realized what he had done—the driver backed up, running over her again. She was pregnant with her ninth child. Both she and the child died."

"What a tragic story! Do you know where the house is?" I questioned as we entered the outskirts of the village.

"I was told about where it is. I think we should turn on this next street."

The house seemed empty, but we inquired at the neighbors, and the man there offered to send his daughter to take us to a little carnival where we found the family. The children were playing on some primitive swings and merry-go-rounds while the half-drunken father stood by the fence watching. "We've heard about the tragedy in your family, and wonder if we can help you," I tried to explain to him.

"I'm sorry, señora, that you found me in this condition," the father managed to say after great effort. "Thank you for coming."

Although he was unkempt, unshaven, and his eyes were blurred and his face flushed, his courtesy and gentle ways with the children impressed us. The children were unkempt too and had only tattered clothing. The older girl was carrying the baby sister, about a year old. Looking closer, I could see that the baby was sick with the familiar symptoms of malnutrition. Another little fellow, about 2, stood nearby with a sad, distressed look. He was obviously sick too, his limbs thin and his tummy protruding.

"May we take you home?" Ken asked the father. They all piled in the back of the pickup. The children went on into the house while we tried to talk to the father. He began telling us about the tragedy, but ended up sobbing and saying vehemently, "I'll kill that truck driver if I can just find him!"

As Ken tried to calm him, I asked, "If we come back tomorrow, will you not drink anymore tonight? We want to help you."

"I'll be OK tomorrow," he promised. "I'll be waiting for you."

When we left we wondered what condition he would be in the next day. "The neighbors say he drinks up everything he makes and the family goes hungry," the director told us.

Ken was dubious. "We'll come back tomorrow, but I'll be surprised if he is there."

When we arrived the next day, however, the children were playing around the yard and the door to the little house was open. True to his word, the father was waiting for us, apparently normal and sober.

The house was really just a shack with just two or three old chairs and a table. The crude kitchen consisted of a cement sink and a built-in type of native stove that allowed smoke to fill the room. The older girl, although thin and small, carried the baby on her hip. She said she was 13, but looked to be much younger. Her eyes seemed wistful as they fastened on us. The family offered us the only chairs.

"Would you like to tell us your story?" I asked the father. "We know you have suffered a terrible tragedy in the loss of your wife."

Through his tears the broken man told about the mother and wife, of the horror they had all gone through the night of the accident, again reiterating his vow to kill the man who did it.

"Do you have work?" Ken asked him.

"Yes, I am a brick mason, and I usually have work, but now the children don't have a mother! Gladis, here," he said, glancing toward the oldest girl, "is doing her best, but she is too young, and she should be in school." Then breaking down again, he sobbed,

"Why did this have to happen to such a good woman as their mother?"

We did what we could to comfort him. Although he obviously loved his children, we could see that, with his drinking problem, they desperately needed help.

"We have a home for children called The Pines, out at Las Lajas," I finally suggested. "It is especially for children like yours." And we explained the program to him. "Would you like for us to care for your children there?"

His eyes brightened. "You are very kind. I don't know if I could stand to be separated from them, but I realize they need better care."

"Think it over," my husband added as we prepared to leave, "and talk to some friend that you have confidence in. We'll stop to see you when we are in town again."

As we stood to go, the older girl grabbed my hand and pleaded, "Please, señora, take us with you now!"

"Do you really want to go?" I asked her.

"Yes, yes, right now," she insisted.

I gave her a hug and assured her, "We'll be back. Don't worry. We'll do what we can to help you."

The next day the father and a friend arrived at The Pines. They had come to look the situation over and to ask more questions. Obviously, the neighbor was strongly advising the father to accept the help we offered.

In a few days all of the children, except the oldest boy, became part of our Pines family. Attending school in the village, he had decided to stay with his father. We took the two little ones to the city. They both needed medical attention and more care than they could get at the local clinic. The father signed papers, giving us custody of his children, and agreed to let the smallest children go with us to the city.

The children adjusted to their new home, and those of school age enrolled in our new primary school. The next time I visited, they came running to meet me. "Mommy Fleck," they shouted. Walking to the house, they clung to me, all trying to tell me about their new home. When she had a chance Gladis sidled up to me. "Everything is so good, we are so happy here!" Relieved of the heavy burden of trying to be a mother, a burden too heavy for her, the girl could now be the child she should be.

Later, walking back to our camper, I told Ken, "The difference that we can already see in these children is a good example of what we can look forward to in the future."

He agreed. With his arm around me as we walked, he said, "You know, my dear, what we have started hasn't been easy, and it is not going to get easier, but when you see what we saw this evening—such a change in these children in such a short time—it really makes all the effort worth while, doesn't it?"

"It really does. When I see the color coming into their cheeks, the light in their eyes, and their happy expressions, I can't think of anyplace else I would rather be!"

11 We Need a Plan

Señora! An army car is stopping out in front!" one of my helpers warned.

We were constantly aware of the nearby army base. Not only was its commander, General Benedicto Lucas, brother to the president of Guatemala, friendly to the mission school, his niece was attending there. It was because of this that we had been able occasionally to travel on the military planes. I saw a white Jeep station wagon parked out in front of the warehouse where I was working. "Could it be the commander?" I wondered.

When I opened the door the commander, himself, stood there. With him were two little girls in typical Indian dress.

"Buenos días, señora," he said politely. "I've brought you some little orphans!"

"Come in, come in!" I welcomed them.

"These little girls have been staying at the military hospital on the base," General Lucas explained. "They are orphans, and I've been told that you are making a home for orphans."

"Yes, that is what we are here for, General. Tell me more about them."

The officer reported all he knew about the little girls. "I don't have their papers here with me, but I will be responsible for getting what you need."

It was obvious that the children were afraid as they clung to the general. Putting an arm around each, I said, "Of course they can stay." Then speaking to the girls, I said, "You can live here with us and have a home. We will love you and care for you. Don't be afraid."

Turning to go, the military leader paused, then said, "I'm happy for what you are doing here, Señora, You can count on me to help you all I can. Let me know if you need anything. You know there are two things that are important to me."

"What are they?" I asked him.

"They are children and animals. I love children and all animals."

Months later I visited with the general to thank him for the many ways he had helped us, such as giving us free rides on the army planes and granting permission for our trucks of supplies to enter the country.

"General Lucas, since we fly back and forth to the States often, is there anything we could bring you?" I asked him.

He thought a little, then replied, "Actually there is. I have wanted a white German shepherd. If you find one, I would really appreciate your bringing it. It needs to be a female to mate with the dog I have."

When I asked about bringing it into the country, he

said, "No problem, just let me know when you are arriving, and I'll make arrangements."

It took quite a search to locate a nice white German shepherd puppy, but we did find one. I bought a carrier for her, and she rode in the baggage department to Guatemala. Because I traveled alone that time, I worried if the puppy would arrive safely. But as I was getting my bags, an airport employee approached me. "Are you Alcyon Fleck?"

When I nodded, he said, "We have a cage with a puppy in it for you. General Lucas sent a plane here to take it to Poptun!"

Later the general thanked us profusely and took us to see his farm and his animals.

After the general left The Pines, I thought, *Army officers are known to be tough, but he must have a soft side to him if he loves children and animals. He is an interesting man.* Then I took the girls over to the director in House 1 and introduced them. When she tried in Spanish to explain to the girls what was happening, she quickly realized that they didn't understand. They spoke only their Indian dialect. *Well, I guess we'll just have to depend on the language of love,* I thought. The director brought out a couple of dolls that brought smiles to the girls' faces. I could see that they would soon be at home.

Later, sitting at the table in our camper, I told Ken, "You know, the first house is finished, and the administration building is nearly done. Both the cottage and the cabin will soon be full. We need to get started on the next house, but we don't even have a plan yet. Both buildings are located on the road."

"That's true," he agreed. "We have about 20 acres in this area that we had hoped to use for our main campus, but it is so thick with brush and trees, you can't even walk through it. We need to make a master plan."

I pointed. "That big hill over there would be a good place to get a good perspective. Is there any way we can get up there?"

"I suppose we can take a machete and cut our way through. It will take a while. Shall we try to do that tomorrow?" he suggested.

"Yes, let's do. We'll wear old clothes and should start early enough to get back before dark. By the way, they say there are poisonous snakes around here."

"Well, we'll make a lot of noise and scare them all away," Ken said, laughing.

The next day, after lunch, we embarked on our project. We would go up on the hill, spot out the land, and make a general plan for the 10 houses, the school, and the church that we would eventually have. Ken borrowed a good, sharp machete and we headed out. We hadn't realized just how thick and high the brush was. The small pine trees were so dense in places that we could hardly get through them. When we finally reached the foot of the hill, we learned that it was a hard, rough climb. Apparently no one, at least in recent years, had been up there. Ken tried to find the best places to cut through, weaving back and forth. Finally, near late afternoon, we arrived. The summit was fairly clear of brush so that we could go to the side overlooking the 20 acres.

"How beautiful!" I exclaimed. "Look! You can see

all over the valley, even the mission school. There's House 1 over that way."

"Yes, and the administration building just to one side," Ken added.

We designated certain big trees to use as a guide. "I've always pictured a road, running around this land below us in an oval, with houses all around the outside and the school and church in the middle." It excited me to think of what the place could be someday.

Ken, a little more practical, helped me to identify land marks that could guide us in the future. "Can you imagine this all being cleared and in lawns?"

"Oh, yes! But the day I am looking forward to is when we will have 10 homes circling the road, each one with its own acreage and gardens, and at least 100 children. It's so quiet down there today, but someday there will be children's voices wafting up this way."

It was a special moment that we would never forget. The sun was getting lower on the horizon, and we needed to start back. But first Ken suggested, "Let's have a special prayer up here that God will bless and that His angels will hover over this place."

12 Miracle Baby

"We have a baby girl here that has been abandoned," a nurse from General Hospital in Guatemala City said over the phone. "Can you take her?"

We were back at the home we had been renting for children. In those early days we found ourselves wearing many hats. Although we had hired a girl to help with the housework, I often cooked, washed diapers, cared for babies, and did all the things that go with a house full of children. My husband helped me in every way he could.

After hearing more details about the baby at the hospital, I agreed to see her and said to Ken, "We need to go to General Hospital. They have a baby they want to give us."

As soon as we could arrange things at the house, we left for the hospital. Someone directed us to the office of the social worker. Apparently the nurse who called us had explained who we were.

"This baby's mother left soon after she gave birth," the social worker explained. "She is a young single girl who said that she had no way to care for the baby and wanted us to find a home for her."

"Do you know where she is?" I asked.

"Yes, she is a maid in a home. You can talk to her."

The social worker took us to the nursery to see the baby. "This baby was born prematurely," the woman explained. "She still weighs only five pounds, but she seems healthy."

When I watched through the nursery window as a nurse lifted the baby from the crib, I noticed to my dismay that the infant had been lying on a black rubber sheet. I knew that the government hospital was always crowded with the sick who couldn't afford private care. I had even heard that sometimes patients slept two to a bed, or that people even slept on the floor. As the nurse brought the baby to us, I looked at her little face and my heart went out to her. "Such a little mite of a thing," I said to my husband, "coming into a world where no one wants her! Well, we want her!"

We needed to find the mother and arrange for her to sign a release with a lawyer. "The easiest way would be for you to bring the mother here," the social worker suggested. "She can check the baby out of the hospital, and then she can ask you to care for her while the legal work is being done."

My friend Maria Feldmann had offered to help us when needed. She went with me to consult the lawyer and make arrangements with the young mother. In a few days we brought the little bundle home. We had already purchased some cribs, and soon had the newest and youngest infant bathed, dressed, and placed in soft flannel blankets in our nursery.

But I had just gone to bed when our new baby began to cry despite the fact that we had just fed and changed her. "I wonder what her problem is," I told my sleepy husband.

Actually, I never got back to bed. Our baby was sick and I knew we had no time to lose, because she was so small. We took her into the emergency room at the American-style private hospital. They kept her a few days until she seemed well enough to come home. But I realized that I was over my head, with no one to help with such a tiny baby. Quickly we hired another girl, this time an older person with some experience. Still, I wondered how I could do all the things I needed to do with this fragile little one to care for.

Then I remembered a young couple, Heather and Les Leno, who had asked us about adopting a baby when we were in Vancouver. Since I had their number, I phoned them. Heather was ecstatic.

"The only thing is," I told her, "this baby is so little, and I don't have enough help. If you would like to adopt her, could you come down and care for her while we arrange the legalities?"

"I'm sure I can," she answered, "but I need to talk to Les. I'll call you back."

In a few days Heather arrived and took over the care of her baby. Ken and I were expecting several members of our International Children's Care board in a few days. We would be taking them out to The Pines. But I felt comfortable in leaving the new woman we had hired in charge of the children, along with Jovita, the other helper. Heather would care for the baby.

We were gone a few days. The night we returned with the group of board members, Heather met us at the door in tears. "Oh, Mrs. Fleck! The baby is so sick! And the doctor says that she has salmonella and has also had meningitis in the hospital. He says I should go home and forget her. She won't make it!"

No one at the hospital had told us about the meningitis. The news dismayed and frightened me. *What shall I do? O Lord, please help us!* Somehow I tried to comfort and encourage Heather. "Don't give up. God can help us through this."

That evening, after telling our visitors about the sick baby, we all gathered for worship in the living room. I brought her, wrapped in her blanket, and placed her on the coffee table. "We are going to have a special prayer for this little one that Heather is calling Heidi," Ken explained. "Let's each one of us pray, asking God to spare her life and make her well."

Tearful prayers went up to heaven that evening. I couldn't sleep, trying to figure out what we should do. I knew we had to get another opinion. But we hadn't been in Guatemala City long enough to know what specialist to call. As I was praying, I remembered meeting the director of a small agency operated by an American woman that did adoptions. As soon as it was morning I telephoned her. "Do you have a pediatrician that you can recommend?" I asked. Then I told her about little Heidi.

"Yes," she replied, "I have found an excellent young specialist who has studied in the United States. He won't give up. This doctor is interested in every baby. Unfortunately, some doctors aren't that interested in orphans."

Calling his office, I made an appointment for that morning. Heather and I took the baby to see the new doctor, who happened to have his office right next to the hospital where I had taken the child before. He examined her carefully and took some specimens for the laboratory. "We will send these to the lab now, and ask for the results right away. You can wait here."

Finally the doctor called us back in. "This baby is sick all right, but we aren't going to give up on her. We'll find out what antibiotics she can tolerate, then we'll put her in the hospital and do all we can."

"God will help us, Heather," I assured the young woman. "Don't lose hope. I believe this young doctor knows what he is doing."

Heidi did respond to the new medicine and continued to improve. When we had all the paperwork taken care of, Heather was finally able to take her baby home. But soon after arriving, the salmonella reared its ugly head again. Recurring illness constantly plagued her. Finally, after a brain scan the doctor told the couple, "This baby has severe brain damage. Obviously, she had meningitis at the hospital where she was born. She will be severely retarded both mentally and physically."

Although the news devastated the Lenos, their faith sustained them. They had prayed their baby through so much already. "God gave her to us, and we will love her, no matter what," they said.

At 18 months they faced another crisis when they took Heidi, desperately sick, to Children's Hospital. Her fever was out of control. The doctors despaired of her life. Again, the young parents went to their knees, praying that God would save their little daughter's life. Miraculously, the fever subsided, the crisis passed, and she went home cured. To everyone's astonishment, it was the end of her physical problems. Evidently the high fever had cured the salmonella.

At 3 years of age she went back for a complete physical as well as a psychological evaluation. It surprised the doctors. Her records contained the brain scan that clearly showed what the disease had done. "I didn't even tell you how extensive the damage was," the doctor said to the girl's parents. "I can't explain it, but she is now above average for her age." Heather and Les didn't need an explanation. God had answered all their prayers.

Early on, Heidi demonstrated a talent and love for music. Since they are a musical family, the Lenos were even more sure that God had meant her for them.

At the parent-teacher conference during her first year in school, Heather mentioned the brain damage. "She may have some learning disabilities."

"You've got to be kidding! She is the smartest one in the class," the teacher responded.

We told this story at an Adventist-Laymen's Services and Industries convention. At its close the spotlight shone on a grand piano, and Heidi, then a young teen, breezed through a Sonata, her fingers flying. A standing ovation followed her performance.

Heidi has been an outstanding student, a leader among her peers, and a spiritual leader as well. It goes without saying that she is the pride of her parents' hearts. Her goals are ambitious, but anyone who knows her has no doubt that she will reach them.

She has graduated from college with a degree in health science and plans to go on to become a physician's assistant. She has been an assistant in anatomy and physics labs as well as teaching skiing. Her mother just told me how tenacious she is with whatever she goes after. Mrs. Leno also described how she thanks God every day for Heidi. Until recently I hadn't known how much Heather had wanted a baby. "Lord, please let me know if this will happen," she had prayed one day, "or if I should forget it." The next day I phoned her from Guatemala. The Lenos believe that God meant Heidi for them, and I believe that too. And Heidi believes that God had a special plan for her life.

13 We Need More Room

*T*here's a beautiful moon out there. Why don't we go for a walk?" my husband suggested one night as we finished our supper in the camper.

"That's a great idea!" I answered, putting away the last of the dishes. Soon we were on our way. We had parked the camper on a private road belonging to the mission, and we felt safe on it at night. The only cars coming in were either for the mission school or The Pines. Wild animals did live in the jungle, but mostly in the undeveloped area on the other side of the river. We had never heard of anything but snakes on our side.

"I've been thinking about the promise you made before I took on this project," I began as we headed down the road. "You told me you would help me for a year. The year is long past yet you haven't mentioned it."

He shrugged. "Actually, we've been so busy getting the construction going, taking care of all the finances, as well as preparing for new children, that I haven't really thought much about it," he answered.

"Well, that's good news! I can't imagine how I would

manage without you. I don't think Bob really thought about all the issues when he asked me to do this."

"Don't worry about it. I won't leave you in the lurch. Besides, I'm afraid I'm getting about as hooked as you are with these children."

Ken was always good with children. Now, with these little abandoned ones who needed someone so much, he soon responded to "Poppy Fleck," as they had started calling him. They called me "Mommy Fleck." We spent as much time with them as we could, both in the city and out at our children's village in the jungle.

"By the way," he continued, "I just had word that Job and his family will be arriving tomorrow."

Job Castanaza was the son of a faithful layman who was active in one of our districts when Ken had been the president of the Guatemalan Mission. Although he had been just a boy then, Job still remembered my husband and was eager to be involved in our venture for children. He was a welder, builder, and general handyman.

"That will be a blessing to have someone to handle the construction and maintenance," I added. "He and his family can live in the new director's apartment for now until we can arrange something else for them."

"We have enough money now to begin the next cottage," Ken suggested. "As soon as Job is settled in, we'll get him started on it. First of all, though, we'll need to put in a road, at least up to the first site. Jim Bechtel told me today that we can borrow the big old grader from the school to make the road—that is, if they can get it working." The equipment at the mission school had all been donated, and some of it was of rather ancient vintage.

"We're running out of room in both of our homes, so we really need the next house," I told my husband. "In fact, a new little boy was brought today. He's only 2 years old and so thin and malnourished. His mother is a bar girl in town. I guess she tried to keep him, but it just didn't work. I feel sorry for some of these mothers. I don't think the girl really wants her job, but it is probably the only thing she could find."

"Well, I think that construction will go faster and better now with Job on the job. He's a dynamic young fellow."

By the time the grader was available and Job was ready to make the road, Ken had gone to take care of business in the city. One morning Job showed up at the camper. "Señora, I'm ready to start on the road. Since Pastor Fleck isn't here, would you show me where it should go?"

"Yes, Job. I'll be right there." I put on some work slacks, old shoes, and a straw hat. My husband and I had planned the road that day up on the hill. I had even drawn out the master plan.

Probably it wasn't the standard way to cut out a road. Job drove behind me with the old grader chugging away as I walked through the brush, marking out the route. Soon we had the road cleared around the circle of our proposed campus, and it is the one we use to this day.

Back in the city we found our house filling with children, mostly babies. The two youngest children of the group of seven whose mother had been run over were there, as well as little Anna. Every time we came from The Pines we found more children. My friend Maria from our mission days offered to help us part time. She was a lifesaver for me, doing a lot of the legal documents necessary, and helping to supervise the home when we were gone.

One little fellow turned out to be a problem. The handsome little 5-year-old impressed me, "But he doesn't look like an orphan," I told Maria. "He is healthy looking. Why is he here?"

"It's an unusual case," she explained. "His father came to us, requesting that we take him. His wife died in a car accident. The boy had been adopted by them in the first place. Maybe because of the trauma of his mother's death, little Victor was too much for the maids the father hired. I rather think he had another wife in mind too, but I'm not sure. He even signed him over to us. Maybe I made a mistake. The girls here say they can't handle him either."

While we were there, both Ken and I worked with Victor. I sensed that the child was frustrated and rebelling against the drastic changes in his life. We tried to show him love and attention, but we also had to find a way to control him. One day we caught him trying to poke out the eyes of one of the babies. "Ken, I think you need to help us on this one!"

Getting up from his desk, my husband called Victor to him, then pulled up a little chair beside him. First Ken talked to the child, letting him know he couldn't do things like that. "Now, you sit here by me for a while," he instructed the boy.

Victor sat down but not for long. Soon he jumped up. Ken grabbed him by the collar and sat him back down. In a few moments Victor was up again. This time Ken sat him down more firmly. Although the child stayed in the chair, he began to cry. Aware that the maids had beaten him unmercifully but to no avail, we had determined that we would not paddle him.

That evening in worship we gathered all the little ones around us. Ken told them a story, and then helped the bigger ones to begin learning the twenty-third psalm. Extremely bright, Victor learned it quickly. All at once he climbed up on Ken's lap and took my husband's face in his hands. "Poppy Fleck, I need a poppy. Won't you please be my poppy?"

Amazingly, we had no more serious problems with Victor. One day we took the children all for a ride. Victor insisted on sitting on my lap. As we went over an old bridge, he looked down to the stream far below and said, "He leadeth me beside the still water." Tears filled my eyes as I realized this little boy's need for love and acceptance, and also the potential these children have for accepting, so quickly, the love of Jesus.

Out at The Pines construction continued. When we had House 2, it was time to plan for Houses 3 and 4. Our mailing list was growing, and God was blessing. The children in the cabin at the river had moved to House 2, and it was already overflowing. Now we realized that we must have a school. Some of the children were of school age. "We could use the extra room at the administration building," I suggested to Ken, "but what about a teacher?"

"How about Juana Ixot?" he said. "You know she is a teacher with a degree."

Juana had lived with us while she studied at the college in Costa Rica. She had helped me with the little abandoned children I took in, and one day she announced, "I'll help you, Mommy Fleck, if you ever start an orphanage."

"That's a great idea!" I said to my husband. "She loves children. Let's see if she might be available."

The young woman did a fantastic job the first year. When our temporary director left, she was a natural to replace her.

"Juana," I told her one day, "we believe that you would be a good director. What do you think? Would you be interested?"

She didn't feel qualified, but with encouragement, she stepped into the position. Soon we saw that she was the stability we needed there. As the program grew, Juana threw her heart into her work. We became more and more confident of her ability, and were able to be gone from The Pines for longer periods of time.

14 Rumblings of War

Whenever we were in the city we began to notice in the newspaper more and more stories of kidnaping, massacres, and terrorism. The local government and political figures seemed to be the main targets. The political situation became tense. Along with that, our growing population of children made it obvious that we needed more room. One day, after noticing a "For Rent" sign up the street, I discussed with Ken an idea that had been brewing in my mind.

"I think it would be a good idea for us to turn this into a house for children, and to rent another house for our office. Because of the tense political climate, and with so many Americans being at risk, it might be better for people not to think of our other house as an American project. Besides, there really isn't room to keep a big bedroom here for ourselves with so many children flooding in."

It proved to be a good idea. The rent for the house up the street was reasonable, and it had room for an office as well as guests or even more children if need be.

Marta, a girl who had worked for missionaries during our previous service in the country, had asked me for a job. She could take care of the house when we had to be gone, and keep things up.

One day when Ken came in from an errand to the union office, he told me, "Lon Cummings has been kidnaped."

Lon was a self-supporting missionary who had founded a naturopathic clinic in a nearby village. "Why would they kidnap him?" I questioned.

"They don't know many details yet. I suppose it was because he is an American, and people think that all Americans are rich."

Later we discovered that his kidnappers were demanding a huge ransom for him. Every day more news of this type appeared in the newspapers. However, we felt that we were in no immediate danger. After all, we were there to help children. Our daughter, Carolyn, had been planning to visit us. When we had the date set, we began to make plans to make her stay interesting. We decided to invite a number of young adults from the local church, who had been children with her while Ken was president of the mission, to a party that we would have for Carolyn.

The event would take place on a Saturday night. Old friends filled the room. One of them was a young woman named Marina, who introduced her husband, a congressman in the national assembly. Before long the conversation drifted to the tense political situation. "Do you worry about your safety?" one of them asked the legislator.

He shrugged. "I suppose I should worry, but I just

take one day at a time. If it is my time to go, maybe some assassin will pull a gun on me." We wondered at his lack of concern.

Most of the guests left early, because of the danger on the streets at night, but Marina and her husband lingered. They seemed to want to visit. "We travel on the army planes out to Poptun. Is that a good idea?"

"There probably isn't much problem with that," he answered, then added, "You have probably noticed that you never see priests or nuns on those planes."

"Why would that be?" Ken asked.

"There is a reason. Even though most people here are Catholics, at least in name, the government doesn't like the Catholic Church's interference in politics. In fact, I would say that Seventh-day Adventists might be among the most approved group, since they have a policy of not messing in politics."

"Well, that is true," I explained. "We have a philosophy that we should respect whatever government is in power."

Before they left, we invited the congressman to visit our facility in Poptun.

A week later Ken rushed into my office with a newspaper in his hand. "Look at this! 'Congressman Assassinated!' It is Marina's husband!" We could hardly believe it.

Both of us attended the large funeral to let Marina know that we shared her grief and were praying for her. Heavy security surrounded the funeral as many of the guests were government people. Driving back to the house, my husband and I discussed the recent events. "This is looking more and more like a civil war," Ken commented.

"I think we should do something about the camper," I said. We knew it shouldn't stay over at the other house, because it was a definite statement that Americans lived there.

"The only problem is that it won't go under the covering to our entrance at this house. Since we're leaving for the Dominican Republic this week, I'll figure something out when we get back."

Ken had brought a travel trailer from the States in a caravan of trucks full of supplies for The Pines and the mission school. Job had then put in a cement platform for the trailer and built a cover over it. Ken and I planned to use the trailer for our home when we were at The Pines. Not needing the camper, we drove it back to Guatemala City.

"Do you think it is safe to leave the camper there while we're gone?" I asked.

"A few more days won't make much difference. I'll take care of it as soon as we come back."

The International Children's Care board was looking into the possibility of starting another program in the Dominican Republic. Having been missionaries there, too, we knew of the great need to care for that country's abandoned children. Our trip to the nation would be a preliminary one to pursue the possibility of obtaining land, as well as discussing the plan with local denominational leaders and government authorities.

We left Guatemala for the Dominican Republic, planning to be gone a short time. Maria would be in charge until we returned.

15 Escape!

*T*here is a call for you, Pastor Fleck," a secretary told my husband. We were in the Seventh-day Adventist conference office in Santo Domingo. Our report was ready to take back to our board, and we planned to leave the next day for Guatemala City. "It is from Guatemala. They say it is urgent. Actually, they have called two or three times already."

We both went to the phone and, as Ken answered, I stood close by him, eager to know what was going on. He turned to me. "It is the nurse at the center. She says we should not come to Guatemala. The kidnappers are looking for us! What shall we do?"

"Tell her to call back in a few minutes," I suggested.

When he hung up the receiver, we just looked at each other for a moment. Then I began asking questions. "Did she give any details? Where did this information come from?"

"She didn't know many details, but she did say that someone from the union office had phoned her, telling her to give us that warning."

Ken had asked her to phone back in 10 minutes, and

that wasn't very long to consider the stakes involved. Should we go or not?

"There is the problem of getting money to them down there, especially to Juana," I reminded him. "We can't leave them in the lurch with all those children."

Ken had an idea. "How about not telling the nurse, or anyone, our plans," he suggested. "We could fly in, then check in at a hotel until we find out more about the situation?"

With that in mind, we went ahead with our plans. Americans weren't traveling much to Guatemala in those days, because of a travel alert from the American Embassy. Since no one would know us at the airport, we decided to risk it.

On the flight from Miami to Guatemala City we discussed our precarious situation. We didn't really want to go to a hotel when we had a good house with food and a maid. "Let's call Marta from the airport," I said. "We can ask her to be at the gate to open it for us, and not to tell anyone we are coming. I know we can trust her." All of the homes in that area had walls with gates that everyone kept locked.

"I'm willing to try it, if you are," he smiled. "This is a mission adventure we didn't really bargain for! But seriously, we are on God's business, and we can expect Him to take care of us."

We had no problems getting through customs in Guatemala City and quickly found a pay phone. "¿Hola, Señora, donde esta ["Hello, señora, where are you?"]?" Marta answered.

"Marta, listen carefully. We're at the airport and will

be taking a taxi home. Please wait for us at the gate—and don't tell anyone you have heard from us."

"*Muy bien, señora. No tenga pena* ["Very well, señora, don't worry"]."

Marta was a little bit of a woman in her early 40s. She went about her work quietly, very seldom speaking unless spoken to. Her loyalty and responsibility were of the highest caliber. When the taxi drove up to the gate, it opened immediately. The driver gave us our bags and left. We slipped into the house and locked the doors.

"Sit down for a minute, Marta," Ken said, "and we will explain why we came in like this."

We told her about the phone call and our decision. "We won't tell anyone we are here until we know what is going on. You can answer the phone as if we aren't here," I instructed.

It was an interesting feeling to be like prisoners in our own house. We didn't even go out in the yard. Since it was a two-story house we would run up and down the stairs for exercise and even got to chasing each other around the house! We would end up roaring with laughter, and Marta had to laugh too, when she saw her two bosses acting so undignified.

Eventually, we began to make telephone calls to get information, still not telling where we were. Maria Feldmann, a Guatemalan friend from our mission days, was working part time for us. She made regular visits to the children's center to supervise the nurse director, arrange the legal work for the children, and do their shopping. We hadn't contacted her yet, and neither did we want the nurse to know we were home. For some reason that we couldn't quite put our finger on, we didn't completely trust her.

One day, after visiting the children's home, Maria stopped by to see how Marta was doing. When we heard her voice, we decided to let her know we were there. She was amazed to see us, but we quickly explained why the secrecy.

"You know, I'm not sure if I completely trust our nurse over there," she commented.

"Why is that?" Ken asked.

"Sometimes it seems that she doesn't always tell me the truth."

Just then the phone rang. It was the nurse, asking for Maria. Her message startled us. "Right after you left, I had a call from some man asking, 'Who was that woman that just left your house?'"

"What did you tell him?" Maria asked her.

"I just told him it was my supervisor."

When she hung up, the three of us sat there stunned. There was an apartment house close by. We wondered if someone was keeping vigil on our children's home from there and why they were doing it. Could it be they were watching for us?

Then we had another alarming phone call from Carolyn in Vancouver, Washington. "Mom! You and Dad must call the American Embassy and ask them for a car to take you to the airport right today. I just had a call from Jim Bechtel. He heard on his ham radio that the kidnapers are after you!"

The situation was getting worse. Finally Ken broke the silence. "Maria, I think you should call the union office and see if you can track this rumor down. We need to know if it is false or not!"

Maria managed to contact the person who supposedly had sent the information. When she hung up she seemed puzzled. "That pastor says he has heard that you might be in danger, being Americans, but he doesn't know of any definite threat."

"But what about that call we just had from the other house?" I asked.

The three of us sat there, discussing various possibilities, not really knowing the truth. "It could be a false rumor," Maria said, "but I don't think you should take any chances. No one knows you are here but Marta and me. I'll do all your errands and phone calls."

"I'm thankful we have you and Marta that we can trust," I told them. And I really meant it!

"One of the first things we need to do," Ken observed, "is to contact Juana. I guess she will have to take the bus and come into town. We need to give her money, and we must prepare her to carry on for a while if we should have to leave."

By the time Juana arrived we had already been "prisoners" in our house for two weeks. Together with our trusted employees Juana, Maria, and Marta we made our plans. First we arranged the finances to conduct the program for an extended time. Maria would handle things in town, and Juana at The Pines. Carolyn phoned again, urging us to depart immediately, but we assured her we were safe for the moment and that we were making plans to leave. We kept in touch with her by phone. Juana stayed there with us and Maria came regularly. The problem was the camper. Since it posed a problem here and we didn't want to lose it, we needed to get it out of the country. We pursued the idea of driving it out.

"But terrorists are killing people on the roads," Maria warned. "You would be a real target, driving that big camper with a United States plate on it. It's a long way to the border, probably a five-hour drive."

"I think I'll call the American Embassy and get their advice," Ken decided.

After talking to them, he hung up and turned to us. "The consul says the danger will be motorcycle terrorists. He said to watch out for someone on a motorcycle or a car following too close. Otherwise, if we stay on the main highway, we probably will make it. The worst danger is here around the city."

Finally we had our plans made. Juana would ride with us to Escuintla, the first town of any size down near the coast. We would leave early in the morning and make a run for the border.

The night before we left, Ken phoned the nurse at the children's home. "Yes, we are home," he said casually, "and we are fine, thank you. But I am planning to move the camper tomorrow since it's blocking your driveway. It will be early, and I have a key, so don't bother to get up." After he hung up, he turned to me. "She seemed glad to know we were home, but wasn't surprised about the camper."

Ken and I packed enough of our things to take with us in case we didn't return for a while. Before daylight Marta fixed breakfast for us and packed us a lunch. We had the suitcases and baggage out by the gate.

"This is the time we need to pray, Alcyon," he said. "Call everyone together."

Marta, Juana, Ken, and I all knelt together in the living room, while he prayed fervently for our safety, for Juana's safety as she returned on the bus, and for Marta, staying alone in the big house to care for everything in our absence. It was a solemn time for all of us, but also a precious moment of faith and unity. We knew that God would send His angels to be with us all.

Ken and Juana walked down to the other house, got the camper, then drove off in the other direction and then around the block. Quickly they backed up at our gate. Ken wore an old straw hat. Marta helped us put the things in quickly. We hugged her goodbye, and the three of us started on our way while Marta quickly shut the gate and locked it. I sat in the middle and hoped that I wouldn't be too visible. Ken drove off in the opposite direction from the other house, and we were on our way. Morning traffic had started already, and we kept a sharp watch for anyone apparently following us. When we reached the main highway, I asked Ken, "What are you going to do if a car or motorcycle comes along side of you in a threatening way?"

"If I see he is going to shoot, I will turn sharp and drive into him!" Naturally we hoped and prayed that nothing like that would happen.

About an hour down the road we went through Escuintla, and at the other end of town let Juana out at a bus stop. "Thank you, Juana, for everything!" we said. "We always know we can count on you."

"Don't mention it," she answered with a smile. "I'll be praying for your safety."

"We'll call you when we get across the border," Ken told her, "and we want you to phone Carolyn right away, so she will know we are on our way out of Guatemala."

As we drove along we felt strangely alone, two Americans in a big camper with a United States license. To say we were not at all nervous or tense would not be the truth, but there was a feeling of peace. We knew that we were on God's business, caring for His children. He would be with us. I sat quietly for a while, thinking over the events of the past months and praying silently, "Lord, You have given me the assurance that this is Your program, that its success is Your responsibility. We are counting on You now. I am so thankful for that day when You told me, 'Why are you so afraid? Don't you know you have a Father who loves you?'"

16 Our Angel Was Busy

We had crossed the border from Guatemala into Mexico many times before, but we were never so thankful to be in Mexico as that day. The drive from Guatemala City had been uneventful though we didn't relax our vigil all during the long hours of that day. Once across the border we headed into the city of Tapachula. After finding a good hotel, the first thing we did was to phone the city center. "Juana! We are in Tapachula! How was your trip back on the bus?"

"I am so glad to hear from you, Mommy Fleck. Marta, Maria, and I have been praying for you. I didn't have any problems. I'll call Carolyn right away. I'm sure she is eager to know you are safe."

Our trip through Mexico was a welcome relief. We had traveled its length at least 16 times during our former years as missionaries in Central America. This trip gave us time to evaluate everything that had happened up to that time and then to plan for the future, even though the fate of International Children's Care in Guatemala seemed uncertain right then.

"Do you think we will be able to go back to Guatemala soon?" I asked.

"It's hard to say right now," Ken answered. "But we have a board meeting coming up, and we need to take another trip to the Dominican Republic to decide on property. We can make good use of our time away from Guatemala."

"Maybe we can put our house in St. Helens up for sale while we are home," I suggested.

Since Ken had retired, another minister had come to take his place. We had purchased a piece of Dad and Mom Fleck's farm near Columbia Academy at Battle Ground, Washington, planning to build a small home there for our retirement.

Our days at home went by too quickly. We had done some investigating of the alarming news we had received about the threat of being kidnaped. Either the rumor had been exaggerated or the danger had passed for the time being. By the time we needed to take more money to Guatemala, we felt comfortable in going back. Ken decided to stay in our home to do some work that would make the house more saleable while I went to Guatemala alone.

Arriving in Guatemala City, I took a taxi and found the house that we lived in well cared for. Marta had kept everything just as if we had been there. "Were you afraid here in the house alone?" I asked her.

"No, not really. This is a secure house with bars on the windows and a lock on the gate. I did have one scare, though."

"What happened?"

"Well, you know that because of the war, police could come and search a house any time they wanted to. One day a group of armed men in uniform demanded entrance. They said they had to search the house."

"Whatever did you do?"

"I went to the gate, but didn't open it. I told them that the owners were not there and that I did not have permission to let anyone in."

"You mean you stood out there by the gate and refused to open it? They could have put a gun to your head or climbed over the wall!"

"They insisted, but they didn't show any written order to search. Finally they went away."

"Marta! You are something else. They could have been guerrillas and not police or soldiers at all! I'm sure God was with you, but you were really brave. I knew we could trust you!"

The nurse at the children's house had proved to be less than reliable. From other incidents we decided that she had taken advantage of the tense situation. After she left and I went to look through the house, I discovered many things missing, including most of our extra bedding.

The atmosphere in Guatemala City was becoming more tense. The headlines each morning seemed to tell of another kidnaping or other atrocity. I knew that the civil war between the guerrillas, or People's Army, as they called themselves, and the regular army was becoming more intense, but most of the fighting took place in the highlands. As I traveled about the city I noticed that I saw Americans less and less frequently. In fact, the American embassy advised tourists and Americans living there to stay off the streets and avoid going into the countryside.

One morning, while alone there with Marta, I answered the phone to hear, *"Señora Fleck, habla General Lucas. ¿Como esta* ["Mrs. Fleck, General Lucas speaking. How are you?"]?"

While we had been on a friendly basis, I had never had a personal call from the General. I couldn't imagine why he would be phoning me, or how he knew our number. I had heard that he had recently become head of the armed forces and now had his headquarters in the capital. "I have two children here in the military hospital that are victims from the war zone," he continued. "I would like for you to see them. Can you come this morning?"

Of course I agreed to go, and before I could think, he added. "I'll send a car for you." Getting the address, he then hung up.

For a moment I felt a sense of panic, knowing that an official car was not the safest mode of transportation at that time. I would rather have driven myself there, but it was too late. I had no way to reach him. In just a few minutes a long black limousine with official plates arrived with two soldiers. One of them ushered me into the back seat.

Possibly thinking that I wouldn't understand Spanish, the driver asked the other soldier, "Where are we supposed to take her?"

Remembering all the people disappearing those days, my heart nearly stopped. Why had I gotten into this car! But then I collected myself and decided, *No, General Lucas wouldn't do that to me!*

They drove me to the big military hospital complex and let me out right at the door of the office. The commander of the hospital was watching for me. "Mrs. Fleck? We have two children here who were brought in after a battle. They were both injured, but are ready to leave the hospital now. General Lucas wants you to take them to The Pines. He says it is the best place in Guatemala and that we are not to send them anyplace else."

Then he led me down some corridors to the nursery unit to where a small girl, about 10 months old, stood in her crib. He pointed to her feet. "Apparently she was on her mother's back when her mother was shot." Part of one foot was gone and the toes on the other one. "The nurses here have given her a name, because we don't know who she is. They call her Mercedes [Mercy]."

My heart went out to the little girl. Fear filled her serious eyes. I began to talk to her in Spanish to get her confidence, then put my arm around her. "The other child is a 7-year-old boy, Lazaro," the military hospital official said. "We believe his family was killed. He had a wound on his head and his hand."

The expressions on the children's faces and the pain in their eyes profoundly affected me as I stood face-to-face with the reality of the war and its effect on these innocent victims. The commander took it for granted that I would accept them. "We'll go back to the office and fill out their papers, and the car will be waiting to take you back." It was that simple! Two little lives and now I was responsible for them!

Back in the limousine Mercedes sat on my lap and Lazaro close beside me. Suddenly the girl began to scream in terror. Not knowing where she was going, she clung to my neck so hard that I could hardly breathe. Lazaro quietly squeezed himself against me.

That night when I tucked him into bed he also began to sob as if his heart would break. I knew he was crying for the mother he would never see again, and from fear of the future. I knelt beside his bed, holding him, rubbing his back, comforting him as best I could until he finally fell asleep. I had to hold and rock Mercedes to sleep. My heart was heavy, knowing that not just these two, but so many children coming to us had suffered what they should never have had to go through—the sudden loss of their parents and the only security they knew. There by the sleeping children, their faces still tear stained, I prayed with tears running down my own face. "Oh, Lord! How can I bring them comfort? How can I supply the love and security that these children need? There are so many of them and I feel so inadequate! You have brought me here. I am depending completely on You."

I received permission to fly on an old military DC-3 out to Poptun with the two children. Job met us at the airfield. When we arrived, Juana rose to the occasion immediately. She was getting used to new children showing up unexpectedly. She took Mercedes to a house where the mother could handle another little one, and Lazaro went into a home that had other little boys his age. I went with her to help the children get initiated into their new homes.

Not long before we had hired Pastor Cruz Ixcot, Juana's brother, to serve as general administrator as well as chaplain for the children. We were growing too fast for Juana to handle everything alone, and she needed a man because of the constant threat from the guerrillas.

Job was busy building houses as quickly as money became available, but not at the same pace as the demand for space. The victims of the war arrived faster than we could provide housing. The housemother in House 4 already had the allotment of 12 children, but when we received three little ones after the civil war killed their parents, she told Juana, "Let me have them. We can't turn away any children."

Besides taking care of the finances, I met with the new houseparents and helped Juana solve the countless problems. A truckload of clothing and supplies had come from Vancouver along the highway through Belize. The commander of the base sent word to the border to let the vehicle enter without the usual inspection. Juana and I spent long, hot hours in the warehouse, unpacking boxes and sorting clothing, bedding, kitchen equipment, and other supplies the houses could use. When it came time for me to leave The Pines, Job took me to the military base to arrange for a flight. I waited in the cab of the pickup while he went into the security office to get a pass. "Who is that woman out there in the car?" the official asked.

"That is Mrs. Fleck. She is the founder and director of The Pines."

"¡Que atrevida! ["How daring she is!"]," he commented.

When Job told me of the remark, I realized that maybe I was a little too daring. But somebody had to do it! I was learning more and more to trust my life in God's hands.

Now that Ken had arrived, we kept busy overseeing the city center as well as the developing program at The Pines in the jungle. We had made the trip between them by car several times, but never knew what we would encounter. The unpaved road was almost impassable sometimes, and we knew that we would be in real danger if we became stuck on the way. Whenever possible, we tried to plan our journeys only when we could find space on a military plane.

We had a trip planned for a Thursday morning. The military base told us that the aircraft would have room for us. A mother of two of the students in the mission school heard that we were going and came to us with a package. "Would you take this to my daughter? It is her birthday."

Of course we agreed to do it. But something unforeseen forced us to postpone our trip for a few days. "I'll phone the woman that we won't be going," I told Ken.

She came by to pick up the package and mentioned that she had succeeded in getting space on the same plane we had planned to take. Later that day we received a call from Juana that nearly made our hearts stop. "Mommy Fleck, the army plane crashed out here just a few miles from The Pines. The weather was bad, and in circling to find a hole in the clouds, it hit the top of a hill. Everyone perished."

It was the aircraft that we had planned to take, and

that poor mother died. It was hard for us to understand why she had perished even though events prevented us from going on that plane. But we were thankful that our lives had been spared. Once again we realized that God's hand was over us.

"Will we have the courage to get on another military aircraft?" I asked my husband.

"I guess if you consider the dangers of traveling on that road, it may be worth the risk. This is the first wreck I have heard of in recent months."

17 This Baby Is Dying!

*B*eth Platner, my sister LaBreta's daughter, had just graduated with a nursing degree at Pacific Union College. Her mother phoned me and asked, "Would you have a place for Beth to be a volunteer? It's something that she wants to do."

Even though there would be some risks, Juana felt they could care for her, and they really did need a nurse at The Pines. Beth came and, with all the enthusiasm of youth, entered into her work. She helped Juana with the sick children. Almost all of them had health problems when they arrived, including that old killer of children in Guatemala, dysentery. Many others suffered from bronchial problems, skin problems, malnutrition, and always, parasites.

One day while we were in the city I received a phone call came from Poptun. "Two little premature twin baby boys, only four pounds apiece, were brought to us," Juana announced. "They were born out in the jungle with no medical care. We have them in the little local hospital here, but one of them is desperately sick. The infection in his eyes has spread into his bloodstream and they can't treat him here. What shall we do?"

After getting more information, I told her to call back in a few minutes after Ken and I had had a chance to talk it over. The only solution was to send a private plane out to bring the child in. Could we afford it? Ken contacted a charter service. "We can't let the baby die!" he said. "Somehow we'll find the money."

When Juana called back, we told her when to meet the plane. Beth would accompany the baby. The doctor arranged for him to have intravenous on the way. We picked them up at the airport, then rushed the child to a local private hospital.

My niece spent most of her time at the hospital with the baby, and within a week he had improved enough to be released. We decided to bring the other little twin to the city also. They were identical twins, and we all fell in love with them. After we had all the paperwork finished and the babies were well, we found adoptive parents in Oregon that were thrilled with the darling little boys. We kept track of them through the years, and when we met them at church gatherings, the little boys would come running up to us. At their eighth-grade graduation I sat there reflecting on those days in Guatemala when we were just a fledgling organization. God had placed the tiny babies in our hands to save for Him. Now they were both class officers, and one of them played a piano solo for graduation.

Soon after we brought the set of twins into the city, we decided that we needed a bigger facility. Maria and I went house hunting and found a large two-story structure in a good area of town. It could accommodate up to

15 children as well as having office space and quarters for us and the staff. Beth agreed to stay and become our director. Her Spanish was improving rapidly, and with a crew of helpers, I felt confident that she could handle it. The staff included Marta (who would be the head cook), a laundry woman, a housekeeper, and nurse's aides for both day and night. The children continued to come to us in the city as well as to The Pines. Those not available for adoption we moved out to The Pines as soon as their documents were finalized and their health stabilized. It would be their permanent home. The two-story house was the beginning of our official receiving center in Guatemala City.

18 Massacre!

Juana had come into the city to buy supplies for the school. We were all at the dinner table when a phone call came from Job. "A pickup with 12 children and their three mothers has just arrived," he told Juana. "They fled from an isolated village where there was a massacre. Just before daylight guerrillas killed every man in the village. These mothers escaped to the hills with their children. After three days without food they found a refugee camp. An Adventist pastor brought them to us. Everybody is in pretty bad shape! What shall we do?"

We left our plates on the table, and Ken and I had an emergency committee meeting with Juana and Beth. "I told him to call back in a few minutes," Juana said. "What do you think we can do?"

"Is there any room in any of the homes?" I asked her.

"No, in fact most of them have more than 12 children already." After thinking for a moment, she continued. "You know there is the cabin down by the river. It's empty now. We don't have any houseparents, though, to care for them."

I came up with an idea. "How about telling Job to ask the mothers if they would like to stay and take care of the children for now? I don't imagine they really want to go back to their village."

When Job called back, Juana told him, "I'll catch the next bus back. In the meantime, find some places in the other homes for the group to stay for a few hours. And please get some help and go down to the Rary house and clean it up. Be sure there are beds in there. I think there are more beds in the storehouse."

When Juana arrived at The Pines she found a bedraggled group still in shock and grief. Everyone co-operated, and the three mothers with their 12 children were soon in a home they could call theirs, with clothes, bedding, food, and safety. It was just a few days before Christmas. "You should have seen those children when we took their gifts and their Christmas dinner down to them!" Juana told me later. "All of our families con-tributed what they could to make these war victims know they are now safe and loved."

The reports of atrocities, of kidnapings, and of miss-ing people continued to escalate. In a way, we felt safe at The Pines to be so close to the army base. But on the other hand, the guerrillas were attacking the army in every way they could. They bombed truckloads of sol-diers and blew up bridges. The more widespread the war, the more children came to us, many of them after having seen their parents killed.

One evening Ken and I were discussing this new situation. "We had no idea that the country would be enveloped in a civil war when we started International

Children's Care, but the needs are much greater than we ever anticipated," I told him.

"It is true that we didn't know, but God did!" he answered. "We will save as many of these children as we can. You know, it is really amazing that with just the monthly letter that you write, God impresses people to keep the funds coming in, even if it is just barely enough."

"But at least it is enough," I added. "No one has missed a meal, and the houses continue to go up. I am reminded again and again that God really does take responsibility for our humble efforts in our service for Him."

19 Attack at The Pines!

We had flown out to Poptun on an army plane. By now the board had officially named Ken director of finances and development, and I was director of children's services. He helped Juana with the accounting and management of finances, as well as supervising Job's activities. My role involved supervising everything that had to do with the care of the children.

Another shipment had come, a 40-foot van full of clothes and supplies. It was a major job to unpack and sort the boxes. Because we couldn't risk leaving them outside, Juana and I worked long hours in the hot, stuffy storeroom. We had arrived on the Thursday flight, one of two a week. The other was Tuesday when we planned to go back to Guatemala City. Juana and I were both immersed in clothing and boxes Sunday morning when Ken came in and said, "I think we need to go back to town today."

"What do you mean?" I asked, surprised. "I thought we were going on Tuesday. We aren't nearly through here."

"But I think we should go. I have things to do in town before leaving for the States at the end of the week." He was insistent.

Although I couldn't understand his urgency, I agreed to stop and get ready to leave. Cruz, the administrator, had agreed to drive us into town. In those days we never wanted to be on the road at night, especially from Poptun to Guatemala City. The road was extremely isolated for much of the way. We wouldn't leave until afternoon, and that meant we would be traveling after dark. I just couldn't understand why Ken felt so strongly that he had to go, even to having Cruz make a special trip.

Juana hurried to fix us a lunch, and we left. The trip was uneventful, and we arrived late in Guatemala City. Early the next morning, I answered the telephone to hear Job's voice on the line. "The guerrillas attacked last night!" Emotion filled his voice.

"What happened? Is anyone hurt?" I felt my heart race with that terrifying news. With my ear glued to the earpiece, fearing to hear more and yet not wanting to miss a word, I listened.

"Not seriously. Juana and Dina [a 13-year-old girl] were sitting on her front porch on one of those heavy benches. Suddenly, out of the dark seven armed people appeared, one of them a woman. They all wore khaki clothes, and they identified themselves as the People's Army. One of them put a gun to Juana's head and asked, '¿Donde estan sus jefes ["Where are your directors?"]?' She told them she didn't know.

"The other guerrillas carried knives, and some had

rifles. One of them shouted, 'Kill her! Kill her! She won't cooperate!' He took Juana by the shoulder and roughed her up and tried to drag her, but she put her feet behind the board that was part of the heavy bench. Then he seized Dina, and Juana grabbed her by one arm."

Job's voice was trembling with emotion, but I urged him to go on.

"Just then the two girls inside the house, along with their teacher, Rodolfo, realized what was happening. He sneaked out the back door and through the warehouse, but the iron door made a racket that diverted the man holding Dina. 'Run!' Juana told Dina. And they both fled into the dark. The bandits then went to the door to go in, but the lights were out. They demanded the girls give them light, and one of the girls said, 'OK, if you will let us out!'

"So the two girls from inside ran one direction, and Juana and Dina in the other, all of them stumbling in the dark. Juana fell down, hurting her leg, and ended up at House 2 with no shoes and her leg bleeding." (She said later that she didn't go to House 1 because the house-father there was a nervous type and she didn't think he would know what to do!)

"Rodolfo went running down the road to the mission school," Job continued. (The school is at least a half mile away.) "There happened to be a meeting going on and the school truck was parked in front. When he ran in with the alarm, all the men and boys jumped onto the truck and went racing and honking down the road to The Pines.

"When Juana got to House 2, the housefather ran up

the road to my house to get help. I knelt down to pray first, and then raced down to the administration building in my truck. But there was no one there. I was afraid the bandits had taken the girls. But we soon found them, and all assembled in House 2."

"How terrible!" was about all I could say. "Was everyone terrified?"

"You can be sure of that. We were all crying. But we were also praying and thanking God that everyone was safe."

"What about the bandits in the house when the girls left?" I asked him.

"Well, when the truck from the school came roaring down the road, honking, they ran into the woods. We don't know where they went, but we locked everything up and kept watch that night."

When I hung up the phone I realized I was trembling all over. I then understood the reason why Ken felt so impressed to leave. The guerrillas were after us!

Ken, Beth, and I stood there trying to digest all that Job had told us, realizing that the war had really come close to home. "And to think that the night before, we were walking that half mile down to the main road in the moonlight," Ken reminded me. "If they had come then, no one would have known what happened to us!"

"And, though we were unaware of our danger, God was taking care of us!" I added.

We spent the next hour or so discussing what our next move should be. "I suppose that Job has reported this to the local army headquarters and General Lucas, but maybe we should call him too," Ken thought out loud. "If guerrillas are operating that close to the base, they need to hear about it. But, on second thought, maybe we should wait until we hear from Job."

We were still at the center in Guatemala City when Job called again a few days later. I answered the phone. "We were attacked again!" he announced breathlessly. "We were headed to market this morning with the pickup full of houseparents to do our weekly shopping. There were two cars also coming behind with staff. When we got almost to Pozo Azul [Blue Pool, a natural spring], the same armed group came out of the bushes and held us up. They forced us all to get out of the cars and lie facedown on the ground in a circle. Then they took all of our money, the funds for food for the week, as well as the salaries of the workers who had just been paid. Also they took our watches and anything of value. Finally, they shot in the dirt and gravel between us. When they let us up, they said, 'Go back home! If you don't, we'll kill you!'"

"Is every one all right?" I asked.

"Yes. No one was hurt, but we had to do something about food for the children for the week. Juana and I decided we had to go back to town and get food, hoping the bandits had gone with their loot. I'm at the telephone office now while she is shopping."

"Have you called General Lucas yet about the other attack?" I asked him.

"Yes, we did, and he promised to search for the bandits."

"Well, call him again, and we'll contact him too!"

As I told Ken about the phone call, we were really

alarmed. He realized that we had to do something. "I'll try to get in touch with General Lucas tomorrow," he said.

As we discussed the situation I wondered what our first move should be. "I'm sure the general will take some action, but the thick brush and trees on both sides of that road out to The Pines has so many places to hide. Just think of the panic our people must feel, stuck out there with no close neighbors and no telephone." Even though the army base extended to the edge of our property, the barracks and offices were seven miles away and close to town. "The remoteness of The Pines out there in the jungle is a blessing in some ways, especially for the children, but it has its drawbacks, too, doesn't it?" I observed. "If this dangerous situation continues, it will be hard to find houseparents and staff who are brave enough to live out there."

"Well, there isn't much we can do from here," Ken added. "I will call General Lucas to see what they are doing, but mostly we will have to depend on God's promises to send His angels to surround our children. After all, that is the best and surest protection." And, calling my niece Beth to join us, we knelt down to place our program at The Pines, and our children, in God's hands.

20 A New Commander

*K*en did contact the commander of the base, and he said he was aware of the problem. "Don't worry about your people out here," he said. "We'll take care of the situation."

We had no idea what measures he would take, but we did know that guerrillas in the area were a threat to them as well as us. A few weeks later Juana told us, "Things seem quiet around here now. There haven't been any more attacks."

"Do you know if they caught the bandits?" Ken asked her.

"Well, one of the army captains told Job, 'We took care of them. They won't bother you anymore.' He didn't go into detail, but we could imagine what happened to them!"

As our paths crossed, Ken and I kept busy trying to cover all of the needs of the growing International Children's Care. Board meetings and fund-raising required our constant attention. ICC had found property near the Adventist college in the Dominican Republic. Part of it was donated, and ICC raised money for the rest. Don Kirkman, from Auburn, Washington, acted as the president of ICC. As an architect, he gave valuable help in drawing up the official plans that I had sketched for the buildings in the Dominican Republic. Ken and I would fly there to check on progress, then back to Miami and on to Guatemala.

It was during one of those trips that we saw the headlines: "Coup in Guatemala, President Lucas Ousted." I took the paper to Ken. "Look! It has happened! There is a new president. I wonder what this will do to our program. We have had so much cooperation from the government, probably mostly because of our friend, General Benedicto Lucas." He was the president's brother.

"I guess we'll soon find out since we are headed there the first of the week," Ken replied. "I suppose there is hope that a new party in government can do something about the civil war."

"This will mean a complete turnover. General Lucas has no doubt been ousted as head of the armed forces. There will probably be a new commander at the base, too. That can have a serious effect on our program there." I was really concerned.

"Well, God is still in control of His program, no matter who is president," Ken assured me. "We'll just pray and leave it in His hands."

To our surprise we were still able to secure permission to fly out to Poptun on an army plane. Job met us at the military runway, and we headed out through the jungle in the little Datsun pickup. "Have you met the new commander?" I asked. "Is he friendly?"

"Yes, he is friendly," Job answered with a smile on his face. "He is Colonel Cabrera. And he says he knows you. He wants you to see him."

"How could that be? We don't know any Colonel Cabrera, do we, Ken?"

My husband shook his head. "No. The only person I ever knew by the name Cabrera was that colporteur when I was president of the Guatemalan mission more than 30 years ago. He was the one who used to play his fiddle and recite poetry, remember?"

I smiled, remembering the man's brave attempts on the violin. "No, it couldn't be him!"

"As soon as you have time, I'll take you to the base to meet him," Job suggested. "You need to make that contact, whether you knew him before or not."

Juana was at the gate to meet us, and, as usual, she had lots of news. House 4 would soon be ready, and the other homes were bulging with extra children. "By the way," she told us, "remember the little boy, Lazaro, that you brought us?"

"Yes, of course," I replied. "What about him?"

"Well, the other day a man came walking in from Poptun with an official letter. He said that he had been told that we had his son here, and that his name was Lazaro. I wondered if it could be true, because I knew they had told you his parents were killed. But I asked someone to bring Lazaro, and I can tell you there was no mistake! He was Lazaro's father. What a reunion!"

"Really! Did he explain what had happened?"

"Yes. He said that the day of the battle he was away on business and when he returned his family was all gone. But someone thought that Lazaro had survived. He had spent weeks tracking him down. When he went to the military hospital, they had a record of where the boy was."

"What a happy ending for Lazaro! True, he lost his mother and siblings, but he still has a father who loves him. I am so happy for him. I suppose he went with his father?"

"Yes, his face just glowed. He had adjusted to his new home here, but there was no question what he wanted to do when he saw his father!"

The next day Job took us to the base to meet the new commander. After going through security, we went to his office. Ushered in, we saw a big man in uniform sitting at his desk. He immediately stood when he saw us and came around his desk, stretching out his hand, "Pastor and Mrs. Fleck! I am so glad to see you!" Then, seeing the puzzled looks on our faces, he went on. "I'll never forget you! Remember the family you visited years ago, the one with the mother who had tuberculosis?"

Suddenly, my mind went back to our early days as missionaries in Guatemala. Young and inexperienced, I had learned just enough Spanish to get by. The central church had named me as Dorcas leader. One day the pastor's wife told me about a family of 11 children. "The mother is very sick. I think she has tuberculosis. They are desperately poor, and the father is colporteuring in a distant village."

While Ken was on a trip to the interior one day I took the car and went in search of the colporteur's family. When I entered their humble home, I saw a scene that tore at my heart. The pale and frail little mother, just 38 years old, was doing her best to care for her big family while coughing and spitting up blood. She slept with the youngest, a little 2-year-old girl, on a cot in the corner. The oldest child was a 13-year-old girl, Dina, who was her mother's helper.

I insisted on taking the mother to the free tuberculosis clinic. She needed to get into a hospital for care and also to keep from infecting her children. Parking the car, I saw a long line of people extending out into the street. Realizing that I could not leave the mother in the car too long, I went to the head of the line, ignoring the guard who stood there, and walked past him. Going down the hall, I found the sign for "Director." The doctor seated there looked up in surprise since no one had announced me. "May I help you?" he said.

When he heard my story he told me, "Señora, can't you see the line of people? There are 300 people waiting for a bed in the hospital." He looked up the mother's file, as she had obviously been there before. "This woman has waited too long. Both lungs are infected."

"But, Doctor," I insisted, "she has a house full of little children and is sleeping with the baby. I can't take her back there. She is out in the car. I'll have to stay here until you find a way to admit her into the hospital!"

Apparently realizing that I was serious, he handed me an admittance slip for the hospital. I drove her back home and helped her gather a few things to take with her. Then with tears in her eyes she told her children goodbye. My eyes were full of tears too. Just as we turned to go, she saw that the youngest had been playing in the water. "Please change her clothes, Dina." It was her last words to them. She died three months later in the hospital.

At that time we lived on the outskirts of town with about two acres of land. Because milk was hard to come by, we bought a Holstein cow. She provided plenty of milk for us, and some to give away. We went by the Cabrera home regularly to see how Dina was doing and to bring them milk, bread, and other things.

Now I looked at this army officer with wonder as he told us, "I was one of those little boys. I'll never forget you. You were there during the darkest days of my life!

"What can I do for you?" he asked. "Just anything! I'll do whatever I can."

We visited with him for a while, asking about his family and telling him about our program for children. He gave us each a hug as we left.

As we drove back through the jungle to The Pines a sense of wonder and gratitude filled us. But we were also awed with another thought that I voiced out loud. "Ken, do you realize that God knew about International Children's Care long before we did? How could this have ever happened? How could this man have been put right here at this time? This just cements the conviction we have had that ICC was not our idea, but God's. He knew there would be children that desperately needed our help!" Little did we know at that moment what a roll this man would play in the scheme of things.

21 Mr. Voice and Vote

"You know, I thought that the biggest problem we would face in International Children's Care would be the funding," I told my husband as we sat on the patio of our trailer one day after lunch. "Now Juana has been telling me about the problems she is having with houseparents."

"What kind of problems?"

"Well, I think we have some good houseparents who are doing their best. But there seems to be an element that is stirring up trouble. It may even have a ring leader. You know the housefather in House 3 seemed like such a godsend at first. In fact, some of the parents thought he would be a good spiritual leader or sort of a pastor for the rest of them. But something is causing Juana to have doubts, and actually, I have had some concerns too."

"What do you mean?"

"For one thing, when I visit in the homes, the children usually spontaneously rush out to meet us with lots of smiles and happy faces. House 3 was that way, too, until this man came. Now, when we walk in, instead of the children running to meet us, they are all sitting around the room in chairs, looking serious. There is something wrong, and we need to find out what it is."

"I notice you have a staff meeting tonight," he commented. "What do you have on the agenda?"

"Juana and I have been discussing this. She feels that there is an undercurrent upsetting things. Something just isn't right. Some of the women are hesitant to talk. Tonight we will deal with discipline problems, health issues—that kind of thing. Maybe something they say will give us a clue. Juana does think that there is some jealousy about one of the families. She has had to spend quite a lot of time with them because of some of the children's problems and has sensed something going on."

During Ken's ministry I had never even been part of a church board or a mission committee. I felt inadequate to chair a meeting. But early on Ken insisted that, since I was the director, I needed to conduct the meetings and be the leader. So far I had never really run into a serious problem.

The meeting took place in the schoolroom. All the houseparents and teachers were there. After I had opened the meeting and begun to introduce the subjects we would discuss, the housefather from House 3 stood up and asked for the floor. When I asked him what he had in mind, he began to berate Juana, insisting that she was favoring one specific family and that this family should be fired. As soon as he took a breath, I interrupted him. "Señor, this is something that we can discuss later. It is not appropriate to do it here. Please sit down."

As he sat down begrudgingly I knew that he was

angry. We went ahead with the agenda, and no one else objected. Later I learned that he had arranged what he thought would be a "boycott," believing that the rest would support him. At the end of the meeting he came to Ken and I and announced, "Since I have no voice or vote here, I am resigning my job."

The houseparents had all agreed that they would always give notice before quitting so as not to leave a house full of children unsupervised. Somehow, God gave me the words to answer him. "Well, if that is your desire, we will accept your resignation," I said. "We will arrange to take you to the bus tomorrow."

My reply took the disgruntled man by surprise, leaving him speechless. He just walked back to his house. But early the next morning he came to find us. "I've decided that we will stay after all," he declared.

"We're sorry," Ken, who was with me, told him, "We've already made other arrangements. You should get your things ready to leave."

None of the other houseparents commented about the incident. However, we did learn that he had expected that they would all resign at once. His departure seemed to resolve the problem. After "Mr. Voice and Vote," as we always referred to him later, left, peace once more returned to The Pines family.

But it had been a stressful experience for Juana. She was still young and inexperienced in leadership, but we both felt that she had the makings of a good director. She was very good with the children, both in loving them and maintaining discipline. Most of all, she was dedicated to the program. "We need to pray for Juana,"

I told Ken. "With so much responsibility, she is in a hard place."

A few weeks later I was talking to Juana by telephone when she said, "I had a dream that I want to tell you about, Mommy Fleck."

"It must have been an important dream, Juana. What was it?"

"I dreamed that we had heard that Jesus was coming," she began. "He was up on a hill, and we needed to take all the children up to meet Him. We were afraid that we would be too late. You were ahead with the bigger children, and I was trailing with the little and sick ones. I was having trouble making any headway, and you kept urging me to hurry, motioning for me to come. You know, Mommy Fleck, when I woke up, I knew that my dream meant something. I had been so discouraged that I wanted to quit. But now I realize that we are here to get these children to heaven, even if there are struggles. Don't worry about me anymore. With God's help, I'll stay as long as you need me!"

"Juana, I believe that God has sent you that dream," I said, pleasantly surprised. "We all need to know that our only reason to be here is to save these children for heaven after we rescue them from the bad things that have happened to them. I love you, Juana, and I have faith in you that God has chosen you for something very special."

By the time we finished, my eyes were filled with tears. God had encouraged and motivated Juana in a way that I could never have done. As I write this many years later, she has proved her calling. People who

127

watch her in action tell me how special she is, and the children who grow up under her care want to come back to see her again and eat at her table, because she never turns a child away. Just recently, when we were discussing world events and how they could affect our program for children, Juana said, "Beto and I have thought about that, and you can know that we plan to stay at The Pines as long as you need us. We will be the last to leave!"

Beto had come to The Pines as an assistant to Job. He was from Job's hometown, had worked for him before, and Job knew that he was a talented young man who could do many things in the construction line, as well as being a welder.

Juana had joined us soon after finishing college and was still single. As time went on, she and Beto became friends. Since she lived alone in the director's apartment, he took it upon himself to look out for her, especially after the threat of guerrilla attack.

Eventually Juana told us that she and Beto had decided to marry. Since we had been like second parents to her, she wanted Ken to marry them. We went up to the high country of Guatemala to her home to help her celebrate. Now, they could work together for The Pines.

That dream of Juana's did something for me too. It wouldn't be the last problem we would face. But I could always know that even though we had difficulties, God always has answers to them.

22 A Special Baby

We had returned to our home in the states for a few days. One day when I answered the phone, my niece Beth was on the line, telephoning from the orphanage's receiving center in Guatemala. "I just had a call from the social worker at the General Hospital saying that they have a case that they don't know how to solve. They have an 8-month-old baby brought in from a humble hut in the jungle of northern Guatemala. The mother had apparently set the little fellow out in the sun while she was busy. A dog came and began to sniff around him. Since he was not wearing a diaper, the dog ended up chewing off his genitals. This must have been a horrible nightmare for him and for the parents. We haven't learned how they found help. But they succeeded in getting him to a clinic to stop the bleeding and eventually he wound up in the hospital here. He is fairly well healed now, but they don't know what to do next. The hospital has no specialist to deal with such a problem. Should we accept him?"

"Oh!" I exclaimed "How terrible! I don't know what you should do, Beth. Give me some time to call some specialists. Tell the hospital we are working on it and will let them know."

Well, I caught my breath. *This is too big for us, too. What shall I do?* Breathing a prayer, I got on the phone and called a children's hospital. The people there referred me to the Oregon Health Sciences University, and they immediately put me in contact with a Dr. Tank, head of pediatric urology there. When I told him about the problem, he was interested.

"I think I can help you," he said. "I have recently done reconstructive surgery on a baby from Columbia. Take some pictures and send them to me. I will be able to tell you then."

Full of hope, I called Beth back. "Accept the baby," I told her. "I've been in touch with a specialist who may be able to help us. He needs pictures and a copy of the child's file from the hospital."

Beth was elated. Wanting to help the little fellow, she followed through and soon the papers and pictures arrived. When I took them to Dr. Tank, I discovered him to be the kind of doctor that everyone dreams of finding. He was kind, understanding, and had a heart to help children. After taking the case to his board, he notified us, "Yes, I will do reconstructive surgery on this baby if you can get him up here. I won't charge, and the hospital won't either."

"Praise the Lord!" I almost shouted as I hung up the phone.

"What happened?" Ken asked, surprised.

"Dr. Tank will do the surgery and *for free!*"

Calling Beth immediately, I told her to start on his

documents. He would need a passport and a United States visa. When Ken and I returned to Guatemala, however, she was still struggling with the red tape. The American embassy would give a medical visa, but Guatemalan immigration was being difficult. They wanted first one thing, then another. "I'm really getting the runaround," my niece said.

Beth had already fallen in love with the baby and did all she could to make him feel loved and cared for. A happy, good-natured baby, he was a handsome fellow. What could we do to hurry things along? Dr. Tank had told me it was urgent, because of scar tissue, to perform the surgery as soon as possible. We prayed about it. *Lord, this is Your child. You know what we should do to get this passport. Please show us.*

About that time we learned that the new government had made Colonel Cabrera the vice minister of defense, and he now had his office in the national palace. Now we no longer personally had to go each time to ask for a place on the military transport planes. "Just call me," he had said, "and tell me when you want to come and go, and I'll arrange it." We greatly appreciated such help.

"Why don't we invite him over here to the center for a meal?" Ken suggested. "Marta is a good cook. He might come." When we contacted him at the palace, he accepted enthusiastically. He and his wife came, and we had a good time talking over old times. At one point his wife began to ask about our program for children.

"Would you like to see our babies here in the center?" I asked her.

"Oh, yes! I love babies!" And we took them back to the nursery. She picked up some of the infants, and then we came to our little special boy. When I told them his story, it fascinated them.

"We have been able to arrange for a specialist to operate on him and restore him to a semblance of normalcy," I told them. "He will do it for nothing, and the hospital won't charge either, but our problem is that your government here won't let him out of the country."

"Why?" the colonel asked. "What's the problem?"

"It is immigration," I began, and then explained the runaround we were getting.

"Listen," he told me, "write a letter to the president and get it to me tomorrow. We'll see what we can do."

The next morning Ken took the letter to the colonel's office in the palace. Then the following morning at 8:00 the phone rang. It was the head of immigration. "I hear you need a passport. When do you need it?"

"I need it today!" I told him.

"Fine. Bring his birth certificate down to us right away, and you'll have the passport by 4:00 p.m."

"This is another miracle!" Ken exclaimed when I told him about the call. "God already has His people in place. We need never doubt His providence, especially when it has to do with His programs here on earth." Besides the miracle of the surgery, we had a phone call in response to the story I had written in our newsletter. "Can that little boy be adopted?" someone asked.

"I don't know," I answered, "but it would be the best for him, so that he would be where there can be follow-up. I know he was born to a very poor family in an isolated village."

A social worker contacted his parents. Even though they loved him, they realized they could never deal with his special problem. It must have been painful, but they released him. Dr. Tank explained that the child would need two surgeries and then more follow-up. Beth brought him to Portland for his first operation.

Since we were out of the country when she came, Marilyn and Dan Patchin offered her their home while she was in Portland. One of our charter members of the International Children's Care board, Marilyn served for many years as a volunteer in charge of our warehouse here in Vancouver. At the beginning we didn't have an office and she had to use an empty building here at Columbia Adventist Academy to store the donated clothing and furniture. Although the building had no heat, she and her helpers sorted the boxes, packed them for shipment, and then helped to load Dave Bechtel's truck to take them to Guatemala.

The surgery was a success though the boy would need another follow-up surgery a little later. In the meantime Beth took him back to Guatemala. Through caring for this little fellow who had suffered such a devastating trauma, Beth learned to love him even more. He became one of her most special babies.

By the time he was ready for the second surgery, all the paperwork had been finished for him to go to his adoptive family. They were with him for that surgery.

Months later, when he was home and well, the father told me, "His pediatrician can hardly believe all that has happened to him. Dr. Tank did such a good job."

Just a few months ago the adoptive father called me. I was eager to know about the child.

"He is a wonderful boy, the joy of my life!" The man went on to tell me about his son's sports activities and all of his achievements.

Colonel Cabrera and his wife were thrilled to know that they could have a part in making a life for our little special baby. And we learned again that when we have problems, God has the answers!

23. Las Palmas

"We need to go to the Dominican Republic," I told my husband. "The first children's house there is nearly finished, and we need to find a director."

"How do you plan to go about it?" Ken wondered.

"I suppose the best way is to visit the mission office and talk to the president. Actually, I've been thinking about Gladys Williams. Remember, she was your secretary when you were president there? She's married now, but I don't know her married name."

We went directly to the new property that we would call Las Palmas [The Palms] because it had a lot of palm trees. The first building was a small house that we used for temporary quarters during construction. Ken and I stayed there. The next day we drove north to Santiago, the site of the mission office. Pastor Alfredo Gaona received us warmly. We had known him when he was the president of the mission in Guatemala at the time International Children's Care was just beginning.

After telling him about our plans to start a program for children in that country, I explained, "We need to find a qualified person to be the new director. We have been thinking about Gladys Williams, who used to be Ken's secretary. We have heard that she is the director of a school now, but we don't know her married name."

"Yes, she is now Gladys Lora, and one of our best directors," he replied. When we expressed our desire to call her for our director, he readily agreed. "I can understand why you would think of her. She has had lots of experience as head of a school. I won't stand in the way of a call. Talk to her. If she's interested, we'll pass on the request."

It wasn't far from Santiago to the village where she was working. "Let's go today and see if we can talk to her," I suggested.

By the time we arrived, school was out for the day and Gladys was in the teacher's house next door.

"Pastor and Mrs. Fleck! I am so glad to see you!" she said as she invited us in.

I began to explain our plans for a children's village in the Dominican Republic. Finally I said, "Actually, Gladys, we are looking for a director."

"You don't have to tell me anymore, Señora. If you want me to help you, my answer is yes."

Her response surprised both of us. "But we need to tell you about the conditions, etc.," I added.

"No, I don't need to know," she insisted. "I'll tell you why. Recently, I had a dream that left a deep impression on me. I felt that God was speaking to me."

We could hardly believe her words. "I seemed to be someplace over near the Adventist university, and I saw a lot of little children. They weren't just ordinary children, but they were abandoned ones. Somehow, I thought that the dream must have something to do with me. I felt so strong about it that I told my husband. We decided that if God called us to do a different work, we would go."

Her husband, Antonio, walked in just then. After the introductions, Gladys explained our errand and her answer. Antonio already knew about her dream. "What is your background?" Ken asked him.

"I grew up on a ranch in the northern part of the island. I would say that farming was my background until I went to school where I met Gladys. Right now I am colporteuring."

A light came on in my husband's eyes. "If Gladys is going to be our director, would you be interested in being our farm manager?"

"Yes, I have always loved farming, but of course I would need to make arrangements with the mission to terminate my colporteur responsibilities."

Before we left they had worked out the transition details and would move to Las Palmas as soon as school finished.

Again, I had a sense of awe. *Another dream! I still remember Juana's. God must know who should be our directors. He really is in this program!* My eyes filled with tears. The realization of God's direct leading gave me a feeling that is hard to express. I lifted my heart in silent prayer. *Thank You, Lord, for this remarkable way of letting us know we are following Your direction. This really bolsters my faith!*

Volunteers were an important part of our program in ICC. It was no exception when Ray and Berta Jacobs, retired longtime missionaries, volunteered their time to come to Las Palmas where he would serve as temporary administrator. Someone needed to be on the job to supervise the construction and take care of business details. They would live in House 1. It would serve as the office until the administration building was ready. Antonio, Gladys, and their niece, Samilin, whom they were raising, would live in the director's house. Gladys would be the director of children's services.

I spent a month helping her organize the program and learn the various policies governing the acceptance and care of the children. She kept a careful account of our every conversation, which she referred to faithfully in the years to come. I drew up a proposed master plan for the nearly 100 acres there and then a plan for the administration complex. It included living quarters for the administrator, office space, and two guest apartments. Don Kirkman would draw up the blueprints. We would employ the same house plan for children that we had used in Guatemala. The children began to arrive as fast as we could build the houses. Las Palmas in the Dominican Republic was now on the map.

24 José

One time during one of my visits to Las Palmas in the Dominican Republic, Samilin, Gladys's niece, rushed up to me. "Come quick, Señora Fleck, Mommy needs you at the front gate!" Gladys had sent her to find me. I hurried out to the gate, where she was talking to a woman with a little boy.

"Since you are here," Gladys said as I approached, "I wanted you to help me with this case. This woman is not the child's mother, and I don't think she has his documents."

"Let's invite her in, anyway," I suggested, "then we can hear her story."

The child's name was José. Such sadness and fear filled his eyes that I instinctively put my arm around his shoulders as we walked into Gladys' living room. He needed assurance. Then, addressing the woman, I said, "Now, let's hear your story."

"First of all, this boy's mother and father were members of my church. There were several children, but José is the youngest. Some time ago his father died with tuberculosis. That left the mother with no real support and the children to care for. You can't imagine the struggle she had, doing anything she could to earn a little money for food and going without herself to feed her children. Soon her health began to fail. Her symptoms were the same as the dread disease that killed her husband. When she went to the doctor, the news was the worst. She also was in the final stages of tuberculosis. Her concern, of course, was for her children. One day she came to me, because we had been friends, and asked, 'If I die, will you be sure that my children are cared for?'

"I didn't know how I could ever care for her children, but I agreed to see that someone took them in. She was such a wonderful Christian mother. Then one day one of the children came running to my house. 'Come quick! Mommy is very sick!' I ran over to their house and found the poor little mother kneeling by her bed, but she was already dead. I knew she had died praying for her children." The woman wiped the tears from her eyes before continuing.

"My husband is not a Christian, and he felt we could not afford more children. I tried to find good homes for them all, but they were separated. Eventually, José was taken to an orphanage in the capital. It was supposed to be a Christian orphanage, but when I went to visit him, I discovered, to my dismay, that it had too many children and not enough food. He was so sad, just a lost little boy. I managed to take him out of there, because I had heard about Las Palmas. Our pastor told us you really do have a Christian orphanage, with individual homes for the children. I am just hoping and praying that you have a place for him."

Gladys watched my expression. Even though the woman with José didn't have a birth certificate or any documentation with her, we did believe her story. "Do you have a place for him?" I asked Gladys.

"Yes, there is still room in House 4," she said. "But what about the documents?"

Gladys was right to ask about that. It is illegal and dangerous to accept children with no documents. Such children could have been stolen or lost.

"He can stay here for a few days," I told the woman. "If you can bring his birth certificate and the death certificates of his parents, then you can sign for him as a next friend of his parents. It will be in front of the judge in town. Then José will have a permanent home with us."

The woman was overjoyed. By the time we took José down the lane to meet his new housemother and the other children, he was ready to stay, and even smiled as he told his protector good-bye.

José turned out to be one of our finest boys. He was bright in school and always responsible. And by the time he was ready for the ninth grade, he had borrowed an old camera and learned to take pictures. Soon he was taking photographs for his friends in school, earning money for his clothes and incidentals. He finished his 12 grades at the nearby Adventist academy and then went on to take computer science and physical education. After graduating from the university, José worked and saved his money until he could purchase a lot near Las Palmas. He bought the materials and built himself a nice little block cottage. In the meantime he had found the girl of his dreams, and when they were married he could take her to their own home.

As the years passed Gladys retired and Samilin was ready to take her place. She has her master's degree in administrative education. Seeing the need to have not only a primary school but also a secondary school on our own property, she succeeded in establishing the latter and even found some grant money for buildings.

José grew up with a love for Las Palmas, and is now teaching computer science and physical education in its own academy. Whenever I think of him, I remember his little mother who died on her knees while praying for her children. He knows that he will see her again when he can be reunited with her for all eternity.

25 A Mother's Last Wish

*M*y husband and I had just arrived for another routine visit to The Palms. Gladys and Antonio met us at the airport in Santo Domingo. Since Ken and I had lived in the area when he was president of the Dominican Conference, we especially looked forward to these visits. The road from the airport to Santo Domingo goes beside the ocean. The beauty of the palm-lined beach, the intensely blue water with sometimes a large ship off in the distance, never failed to thrill us. It was such a contrast to the poverty and misery found in many of the slums of the cities and villages in that country.

As we traveled the hour and a half to The Palms in the center of the island, Gladys brought me up to date on the homes and children. The children's home always had many issues to resolve—construction, hiring of houseparents, etc. "We just received a message from one of the churches here in Santo Domingo," Gladys said. "It is a small church in one of the outlying areas. They have an urgent case of a new member who is dying with cancer. She was praying for two special requests. One was that she could be baptized by immersion. The church arranged to do that, carrying her down into the water. Her other request was that she could know that her children would be in a Christian home. That was why they called us. They want us to visit her soon while she is still able to talk."

"Oh my!" I sighed. "What a sad situation! Of course we must go. Do we need to make arrangements?"

"Yes, I need to let the elder of the church know when we are coming and get definite directions," she replied.

We discussed the problem and decided to take care of it within that first week.

As we neared the city a few days later, Gladys directed us into an area of abject poverty. Dirty, ragged children raced about the unpaved street. Finally, she located the house that she thought was the one. After going to see if it was the right place, she motioned for us to come.

Through the years we had experienced some extremely sad situations, seen places that made you wonder how anyone could live in them, but this one touched my heart to the core. As we walked in the door, I noticed some children peeking around the corners—a toddler and three other children, stair step in age. The main room had nothing but a bed, where the mother lay. As we entered, she tried to raise herself up on one elbow, with a huge smile on her gaunt, pale face.

Introducing us all, Gladys explained, "We heard that you wanted us to visit you."

The young mother, still in her 30s, said nothing about her pain or her fear of dying. With almost a heavenly glow on her face, she said, with some effort, "I've been waiting for you. I am so glad you have come. I want to talk about my children.

"I have prayed for only two things before I die," she explained. "One has already been granted, when my loving church family carried me down into the baptismal water. You can't imagine the joy I felt! Just to know that now I belong to God's family, and that I am in His care.

"Now I have the other request to ask of you," she continued, still with a smile. "I've been told that you have a home for orphaned children, a Christian home that teaches them about God and heaven. That's where I want them. I want to meet them again on the resurrection day." Every breath was labored now, but the smile never left her face. We were all struggling with the tears that we could not control. "I am so glad you came in time! Please take my children!"

I sat on the edge of her bed so that I could hear her better and be sure she understood me. "Sister, we have come here to help you. We will do our very best with your children. I'm sure you know that we need for you to sign a paper giving us custody."

"Yes, I want to do that. I want to be sure they are cared for."

Gladys slid beside me to help arrange for the document. By then we saw that the woman was tiring considerably. Her breathing had become rapid. "We are going to step out of the room for a few minutes while you rest a little," I told her.

She extended a wasted arm that seemed to be nothing but skin and bones. "First, please send my children all in here to me."

We called the children and ushered them into their mother's room, and then we stepped back into the hall. But we could still hear her talking. "Come close, children, I want to talk to you, and I want you to listen carefully." She paused for breath. "You know that Mommy is very sick. Pretty soon I am going to go to sleep, and sleep until Jesus comes. Then He will wake me up and take us all to heaven. These people are Christian people who have a home for you. They are going to teach you how to get ready to meet me." Then she asked each one separately to approach her, and told the child, "Promise me that you will be obedient and good, and learn all you can about Jesus and heaven. Then when I wake up, we can all be together again. Will you promise?"

Through the opening into the room, and despite the tears blurring my vision, I could still see each little head nodding. Neither she or the children had any tears—only us! Now she was ready to sign the papers. We told her we would come for the children in a few days. Since she had mentioned the oppressive tropical heat in her room, we said that we would get her a fan. Then Ken prayed with her as the children still huddled around her bed.

As we drove away that day—all of us still recovering from the emotional scene we had just left—someone expressed all of our feelings by commenting, "Now I know why International Children's Care exists!"

Ken and I had to leave before the children arrived at the home, but Gladys later told me by telephone how well they were adjusting. In just a few weeks that brave little mother closed her eyes in death, perfectly at peace. Gladys arranged to take the children to her funeral, all of them dressed in white.

After hanging up the phone from the call from Gladys about the mother's death, I again relived the trauma of that unforgettable experience. I bowed my head and prayed, "Thank You, Lord, for letting me be part of such a program as ICC. And thank You for faithfully helping us to provide for little children like them and thus be able to comfort a faithful mother such as her."

26 Cries in the Dark

*T*he big house we rented for our receiving center seemed always to be full. Beth Platner, my niece, needed to return home, so we found another young woman, Sandra Taylor, a graduate of Pacific Union College in California, to take her place. She had her master's degree in social work. Since the adoption program was growing, Sandra fit into the program well. She didn't have the benefit of working at The Pines as my niece had, thus learning the language, but Beth stayed on to work with her for a while. Then after Beth left and Sandra was alone as director I spent a few days with her before returning to The Pines.

One day she received a call from the Guatemalan children's court. "The police broke an illegal adoption ring," an official said, "and they have confiscated about 30 children they found in deplorable condition. Could you take some of them?"

Sandra asked for time to consult about it, then phoned me in Vancouver. After telling about the request she asked, "What do you think?"

"How many are you considering? How many can you find beds for? You will need to hire more help, too," I reminded her.

After purchasing more cribs and rearranging the present group, she finally let them bring her 14 new children. They ranged from babies to toddlers. Fortunately, Marta, from our former house, was working as head cook and had a helper who also did housekeeping. Marta loved the children, and since she was the only one of our helpers who lived in the facility, she often helped with them.

Sandra learned that the police had found some of the children in a shack in the poor section of the city with only one woman caring for them. When the police arrived, the woman had gone off to market or someplace and left the babies alone in the house. They were hungry, filthy, and some were sick. Most had skin infections and lice. It was a huge undertaking for Sandra, but she rose to the occasion.

I was asleep in the guest room soon after my arrival when I awoke to a knock on my door. "What shall I do?" Sandra asked when I opened the door. "A bus strike was called this morning, so none of our helpers could get here. Marta and I are alone down there with this house full of hungry little children."

After telling her that I would be right down, I hurriedly dressed and went down to the nursery. Marta had already fixed bottles and food, but the babies all needed changing and bathing, and the little toddlers were literally going wild! As they finished eating, we got them on their little potties. Sandra kept the bathtub going with one little body after another, as I brought each little customer just off the potty. Then the children discovered that the potties slid easily on the tile floor and began having a hilarious time scooting all over the place, reminding me of one of those bumper car rides I had seen at fairs. Unfortunately, some of the potties overturned, and one little 3-year-old hit another child over the head with a little child's chair. It was bedlam, and Sandra and I were tearing our hair out. But somehow we survived that day. The next day the strike ended, and the girls were back at work. What a relief!

While there at the receiving center helping Sandra I also kept in touch with Juana. By now the civil war had become a fact of life that we had to live with and work around. Juana and Job didn't think we should come out there any more than necessary. But they managed to phone me, even though they had to drive seven miles through the jungle to the village of Poptun to do it. On one of these calls, Juana told me about another frightening experience. Beto, Job's helper, had gone to Poptun, returning by bicycle through the jungle after dark. A group of hoodlums, or possibly guerrillas, stopped him, seized what they could, and beat him. Barely escaping, he raced into the children's village nearly frightened to death. He was concerned for Juana, knowing she was alone. A little later they heard cries coming from out in the dark. *"¡Socorro! ¡Socorro! ¡Ayudame* ["Help! Help! Help me!"]!" The staff consulted with Job and Cruz, but felt it wasn't safe to go searching. It could be a trap.

A little later some students at the mission school reported that they had run into strange men and girls in khaki garb in the woods between the school and the village homes. They had encountered the strangers on a short cut the students often took. Also students found evidences of camp fires and of people being in our woods. At the same time, those who lived in the Rary house down by the river told a strange story. Purchasing a big bunch of bananas at the market, they stored them in the outside kitchen. The bunch contained enough bananas to feed all the children for a week. The next morning it had vanished. At first they thought one of the monkeys from the jungle across the river might have raided it. But there was nothing left, not even a banana peel.

With all these strange things happening, Job called the receiving center, and we happened to be there. "We have to do something!" I urged my husband. "I think you need to contact the army. If there are guerrillas in the area, they will want to know." Ken phoned the nearby base commander. "We wondered if some of your troops have been out in the woods in bivouac or training," he told the officer.

"No, we haven't had any activity out there," the commander assured him.

The next day a soldier contacted Juana, as well as the director of the mission school. "We are going to have some activity in your area," he announced. "There will be planes going over you and bombing in the woods. Please keep everyone indoors tomorrow."

"We stayed indoors, all right!" Job reported. "The air was full of planes, and the ground around us shook from bombing. It either wiped the intruders out or scared them away. It has been quiet since."

The next time I was in Guatemala alone, I flew on a commercial jet to Flores, about 70 miles beyond The Pines. It wasn't feasible to catch a ride on the military planes at that time because of the increased fighting in the civil war. Cruz, Juana's brother, met me with the pickup, and I noticed a strange man riding in back. "Who is he?" I asked.

"With so many strange things happening," he explained, "the houseparents didn't feel safe, and we felt we needed protection. We hired this guard to stay right at The Pines day and night. He carries a gun. Now that you are here, we feel the risk is greater, and he is to keep you in his sight at all times." It was strange to see an armed man sitting in the back of the pickup everywhere I went, even when we went to a neighboring property to see some land for sale. While I knew that angels were with us, mightier than any earthly guard could be, I also understood what it must be like to live out in that remote, vulnerable spot with no real earthly protection, not even a telephone. I have to admit that, sleeping alone in our camper right close to the road, it gave a feeling of security to know the guard was out there.

When Cruz took me back to Flores, the guard accompanied us. Since we arrived early, I would have a wait before my plane departed. Cruz needed to go to the village to see about a new tire, so he left the guard with me.

As I walked around the airport, looking at some of the shops, my guard kept me in sight. Then I went inside one shop, forgetting about him. When I came out, he was desperately searching everywhere for me. Not having seen me go in, he thought sure I had been kidnaped. A look of real relief crossed his face when he spotted me.

It was an extremely tense and difficult situation for everyone in the country at that time. Reports of atrocities, kidnaping, missing people, and battles with the terrorists filled the newspapers. It was especially hard for Juana and her staff living out in the jungle with no telephone and knowing that the guerrillas were active in the area. They learned to lean heavily on God's promises and prayed constantly for His protection.

Ken and I lived through the period of uncertainty and danger by relying heavily on God's constant protection. We decided that we would continue doing what needed to be done, not taking unnecessary risks, but trusting in the fact that our guardian angels would be with us. I believed that constantly living in fear demonstrated a lack of faith. Often I remembered the day that God had told me, "Why are you so afraid? Don't you know you have a Father who loves you?"

27 They Took Poppy

*T*he Guatemalan army brought us children on a regular basis. Young people were always victims of the war. Sometimes a family member accompanied the child or group of children brought to us. Such children came with terrible trauma, especially those who had seen a parent kidnaped or killed. Two such children were Milton and his brother. Their parents had lived in the northern part of the country where guerrilla activity was especially rampant. Since their village bordered a river, going to a larger town required taking a boat downstream to the nearest bus stop.

One day the father needed to buy supplies for his business. Milton's older brother, Estuardo, knew when his father was expected and went to the wharf to meet him.

The little fellow stood on the wharf, staring down the river. Finally, a boat came in sight. The child began to wave, feeling sure his father would see him. Sure enough, he saw a man standing on the deck and he knew it was his father. "Poppy! Poppy!" he called, waving excitedly.

His father waved back, and Estuardo went as close as he could to the dock where the passengers would disembark. But just as his father stepped onto the dock, a group of men crowded past the little boy. While one held a gun, two others grabbed the father and pulled him toward a car with its motor running.

Estuardo was frantic, screaming, "Poppy, Poppy! You can't do that to my Poppy!" He tried to run after the speeding car, but it was soon out of sight, leaving a distraught little boy standing in the road.

He raced home to his mother, crying all the way. She met him at the door, alarmed.

"What's the matter, Estuardo? Tell me what happened." But the child was too distraught to talk coherently. Finally he managed to sob, "Mommy! A bunch of men took Poppy away. I think they were going to hurt him!"

Frantic, his mother ran to the neighbors. "Something terrible has happened! My husband has been kidnapped!" she cried. Soon a group of men sped in their cars to the wharf. They reported the incident to the police, who instigated a search.

The young mother stayed in her home, waiting in suspense and hoping her husband would escape or be released. But he was never found. With two children younger than Milton and Estuardo, she found herself in a dilemma. She had no means of support and was far from her family, who lived in Livingston on the Caribbean coast.

Finally, she took her little family and went home. Her people desired to help her, but she wanted to find a way to become independent. One of her relatives, Bernie Coleman, was a teacher at the mission school. He loved to come over to The Pines to be with the children. Hearing about the tragedy, he went to Livingston.

The family gathered to discuss the future of the young mother, now considered a widow. "Why don't you send the two older boys to The Pines?" Bernie suggested. "I know the director and will explain your situation."

Eventually Milton and Estuardo became part of one of the families in the children's village. Milton was 6 years old, and from the beginning he excelled in his studies as well as in behavior.

He was one of the children who wanted to take the public speaking class and even preach in church services. I remember hearing him speak during one of my visits there. He needed a stool to stand on so the congregation could see him above the pulpit. As in everything he did, he gave a sermon that was outstanding, especially for his age.

After graduating from the primary school with honors from the local government education department, he went on to the secondary school and again graduated with honors. Now he looked forward to attending the Adventist college in Costa Rica with his other classmates. But on graduation day he had a surprise. His mother, who had succeeded in getting more education, had found a way to migrate to the United States. When she came to the graduation, she announced that she had succeeded in getting visas for them to go back to the States with her.

"I would rather go on to Costa Rica," Milton told his mother.

"Well, that is your choice, of course," she said, "but

this may be your only chance to go to the States."

Rather reluctantly he bid his friends goodbye and with his brother went to Los Angeles.

Seven years went by before anyone heard from him. Then Juana received a letter telling all about his life. He had joined the United States Navy in order to get further education. Now he was a Fourth Class Petty officer on an aircraft carrier. He gave her his e-mail address, and Juana forwarded it to our office. Rick, our son, wrote him and so did I. Juana sent a copy of his letter to us. When I heard he had been in the Navy for four years, I wondered, *How has this boy done spiritually? The Navy is a very different environment from The Pines.*

The response from Milton was prompt. He wrote:

"Dear 'Mami' Fleck:

"Your e-mail came as a real surprise, sweet for reminding me of the many years I spent with you guys at The Pines in Guatemala, always joyful and rewarding, full of happiness.

"By this letter I wish to express my gratitude for the many kindnesses and everything that International Children's Care did for me and my brother Estuardo. While no words of mine can express my heartfelt gratitude, I want you to know that you are always in my thoughts and prayers. . . .

"Thank you for inviting me to come to Vancouver, Washington. I am certainly looking forward to visiting you next month. I hope that this does not interfere with your busy schedule. . . .

"Last, but not least, I want to wish you the best on your continued mission of reaching out to others. And want to say thanks to everyone who has supported and supports ICC in any way, whose efforts have enriched the lives of many.

"With my love, Milton."

Milton did visit us and it was a real reunion, one of our boys coming home. We told him he would always have a room to stay at in our house. Later he wrote asking if he could stop by for Christmas. He came, bringing gifts for everyone, and a beautiful leather photograph album for me. I was happy to learn that he never forgot God in his years in the Navy. Soon after his visit, he left for the Gulf region of the Middle East on an aircraft carrier.

Recently Milton phoned me after returning to San Diego. Eager to know his feeling about world events after being a part of them, I asked what he thought of the war and international politics.

"Well, Mommy Fleck, it is just like I learned as a child," he said. "This is all foretold in Bible prophecy. I just purchased the book *Last Day Events,* by Ellen White. I'm reading the book *Great Controversy,* too. By the way, I am so excited. I'm going for a trip to Guatemala and The Pines!"

Afterward he called again. "I just can't tell you how wonderful it was to go home again after seven years. I saw so many of my friends," he said. "Some day I definitely want to have a part in ICC!"

Being Mommy and Poppy Fleck to so many kids is a thrill that gets only greater as time goes on. As we see the heavenly Father's hand in the lives of these children, we just have to thank God again and again that He has let us be part of it.

28 Romania

*M*y husband and I always needed to reserve time for certain events. Since public relations and fund-raising were important to the growth of International Children's Care, we always sponsored a booth at the Adventist-Laymen's Services and Industries conventions, as well as the General Conference of Seventh-day Adventists sessions. At the 1990 General Conference session in Indianapolis, something happened that impacted ICC dramatically.

Ken and I had gone back to our hotel after a long day of helping in our booth, attending meetings, and meeting lots of people. In the room we turned on the television to catch up on what was going on in the world. The newscast portrayed the horrible revelation of the hundreds of children in Romanian orphanages and their tragic condition. My eyes glued to the screen, I wondered, *How could such things happen in a civilized country?* But of course we had to realize that this is what had been going on behind the iron curtain with the dictator Ceauşescu in charge.

That night in bed images of those children filled my mind. I found it hard to go to sleep. *We created ICC to help suffering children. Is there something we should do for the children in Romania?* Finally, I began to pray, "Lord, I know there are 40,000 people at this convention, but if you want us to do something for Romania, please help me to find someone from there." I didn't know if the iron curtain had been down long enough for delegates to be able to travel from Romania, but I determined to find out the next day.

The following morning Ken and I entered the huge hall swarming with hundreds of people. Just inside the entrance I saw a group of young men who wore official delegate name tags. As I drew a little closer, wonder of wonders, I saw the word "Romania"! Approaching them, I asked, "Do you speak English?"

I saw that most of them didn't understand, but one of them stepped forward with a smile. "May I help you?" he asked.

"Yes," I answered. "I want to know what the Adventist Church in Romania is doing for the orphan children."

Obviously, the young man, whom I learned was Lucian Cristesco, the ministerial secretary of their newly organized Romanian Union of Seventh-day Adventists, had heard about the orphanage scandal. "Sister," he answered, "we are poor, we can't do anything. Please come and help us!"

In discussing the problem with them further, they suggested that I talk to their president, because they were having a committee meeting there at the GC. I told them where our booth was located, and that afternoon their union secretary, Adrian Buconanu, came by to talk to us. The result was an official invitation to visit Romania to help them with the children.

Within a few months our board approved a trip to Romania to assess the possibilities of starting a program there. We knew that the new government faced a crisis as it tried to upgrade the orphanages and find ways to provide emergency care for children. The ICC board decided that the best approach would be to secure a building that we could use as a receiving center. Later we could make further plans for a permanent village concept as we had in other countries.

I contacted two of my loyal friends and supporters to accompany me to Romania. We knew we could be among the first Adventist women to visit the country after the dictator's fall. Edna Craik, Ruthie Jacobsen, and I boarded the plane for our big adventure. Adventist Development and Relief Agency also sent David Taylor, who would work with us on a possible grant, in addition to assessing other needs. May Chung, representing the 3 Angels Broadcasting Network, was also in the group. The Romanian Union had reservations for us at a first-class hotel in the middle of town.

Edna, Ruthie, and I were on the second floor in what they called a suite, actually a cluster of three small rooms. It had an entrance hall, a small living area, and a bedroom. Pastor Boconanu spoke good English and became our guide and translator. We spent some time at the union offices they had recently acquired. It was actually a former mansion from pre-communist days.

Our main purpose in this visit was to meet the appropriate authorities and secure their cooperation in finding a building big enough and appropriate enough to care for from 50 to 100 babies. We learned that during the reign of the dictator the government had allowed most buildings to deteriorate. In addition, he had confiscated and torn down hundreds of beautiful old homes, then constructed miles of high-rise apartment buildings. The latter contained three room apartments that had nothing more than the barest essentials. At the same time, the government required families to have at least five children—and the mothers had to work in the factories as well as the men.

The gloomy atmosphere from the airport to the city caught our attention. It looked as if no one had ever painted anything, and the people seemed to be all dressed in dark, somber colors. Soon we began to realize and feel what this country had suffered at the hands of a power-hungry dictator and ruthless government control.

Most of the authorities that we met were friendly and eager to cooperate. They told us that the government would give us a building if we stood the expense of remodeling it and caring for the children. The first building we saw held great promise. Someone had used it as a place to care for babies, and it still had cribs and other equipment. (The cutting back of budgets after the regime fell had produced a lot of such buildings.) They allowed us to take pictures of the building inside and out. Then the three of us began to make detailed plans of how we could prepare it for children. The next day was Friday so we made arrangements to continue with our plans the following week.

"There is a meeting at the central church Friday evening," Adrian told us. "We'll send a car for you." Before going to the church, we ate our evening meal in the hotel dining room. A Gypsy violinist was entertaining the customers. Since I had played the violin during my school days, I enjoyed the music and recognized that he and his accompanist were real artists. May Chung had her video camera and took pictures during the meal. Looking around, I saw that we were probably the only foreigners there—at least the only Americans.

The church of nearly 1,000 members was crowded. After the revolution with its restoration of freedom of religion, 60,000 Adventists filled the churches. Many pastors and members had suffered severe persecution for their faith. It was a thrill for us to see the fervor of the people, obviously finding such a joy in worshiping in freedom.

On the way home, David Taylor commented, "They have asked me to preach tomorrow. I think it would be good for you to talk for 15 minutes or so, telling about ICC, and why you are here in Romania." Of course we knew we would be talking through translators, but I agreed to do it. He and May Chung each had rooms on the third floor, and we bid them good night, going down the hall to our second floor room. None of us imagined what awaited us!

29 Robbers

*T*he three of us kicked off our shoes to relax a little before turning in for the night. We were in the bedroom of our little suite when we heard a knock on our door.

"I'll go see who it is," I offered. "I'm closest to the door."

One of our group, who had the key, had not returned it to the door yet, but had put it on the table, so I opened the unlocked door. Two young men stood there and began to talk in Romanian. Suddenly, the tall one pushed the door wide open and entered. At the same time he grabbed me by the throat with both hands. I screamed and put my hands to my throat. Later I wondered if I could ever scream that loud again. At that instant I felt a prick and assumed it was a needle, but in reality it was a knife point. Suddenly feeling faint, I thought I had been drugged.

In the meantime, Ruthie Jacobsen rushed into the room and stood transfixed a little way behind me. Time seemed to stand still. In reality, it must have been only a few moments. Although I don't remember pushing them out, somehow I did. Soon the door, which had been ajar, with the tall intruder at my throat and the other close behind, slowly shut in their faces. I was pushing on the door with them on the other side. Finally the door closed though they were still trying to get back in as I held the knob. Then I yelled for someone to bring the key. Ruthie found it on the table and we locked the door.

Noticing blood on the door, I glanced at my hand and realized that it came from a cut on my finger. Evidently when I reached for my throat at the same time the bandit did, his knife cut my hand. Also I had three scratches on my throat. Ruthie ran to the phone to call the front desk, but the line was dead! As we stood there, wondering what to do, we heard another knock on the door. The robbers were still out there, yelling, "Cops! cops!" Apparently they figured we would open the door for the police.

"What shall we do?" Edna asked, her voice full of fear. "We can't stay here."

"But we have no place to go," I said. "We have to get help!" Then I remembered something from the night before when we had pulled the drapes across the front windows. We had discovered a balcony that encircled the building. Our room was directly over the front door to the hotel. "I'm going out on the balcony and see if I can get help," I told them.

"But they might be out there!" one of them objected.

"We can't stay here all night with no help. They can break the door down!" I pulled back the curtain and unlocked the door to the balcony. Looking over the railing, I noticed that a car had just let out a man dressed in a business suit. "Do you speak English?" I called down to him.

He looked up, surprised. "Yes, may I help you?"

"We have just been attacked in our room. Please get us help!"

"What room are you in?"

When I told him, he went into action. In just a few minutes people congregated outside our door, including the receptionist, the hotel manager, and some police. Almost afraid to open the door, we did, though, and showed them the blood on the door, my finger still bleeding, and the scratches on my throat. And then we told them what happened.

"What did they look like?" the woman whom I took to be the receptionist asked.

"The one who attacked me was tall and thin with sharp features. He had dark hair and black and piercing eyes. The other one was shorter, but I didn't look at him enough to really describe him."

"No one has come in, or gone out the front door," the receptionist said. "Whoever it was must still be in the building."

"We will need you to go with us to search all the rooms, and see if you can identify anyone," the manager said.

When we went up on the next floor we stopped at David Taylor's room. He pulled his pants on over his pajamas and came along with us. Then we stopped at May's room to be sure she was all right. The hotel representatives took us to every room. We went to every occupied room in that three-story hotel but didn't recognize anyone. One room had two men registered as staying in it, but no one was there. I knew I would never forget that evil face, with those piercing black eyes, of my assailant. But I also realized that I could not accuse anyone unless I was very sure.

Before leaving David and May, I remembered that he had asked me to have a part of the service in the central church the next day. "I'm not sure I am up to preparing a talk for tomorrow," I said to him.

"That's OK," he answered. "Just think it over and let me know in the morning what you want to do."

Once back in our room we made very sure that we had the door securely locked. "Don't be afraid," the hotel manager assured us, "we will have guards outside your door all night."

We gathered in the back bedroom, trying to calm down and discussing the frightening experience. I think we were all still trembling.

"Alcyon!" Ruthie commented. "There's been an angel in this room. You could never have shut that door on your own with two men behind it!"

"You know, I guess I was in shock. I'm not sure just how it all happened or how long it took. Ruthie, you were right behind me. Did those fellows walk out on their own?"

"No, Alcyon. I saw that man's head towering above you until you shut the door."

I went into the front room to get my Bible. I needed to read some biblical promises. Opening it, without turning any pages, my eyes rested on a verse that I had marked in red. "Listen to this!" I said as I came back. "Blessed is he that considereth the poor; the Lord will deliver him in time of trouble. The Lord will preserve him, and keep him alive; and he shall be blessed upon the earth: and thou wilt not deliver him unto the will of his enemies" (Ps. 41:1, 2).

"The Lord has given us a verse!" Ruthie almost shouted.

The rest of the evening we continued talking and praising God. I remembered other times when I knew that God had sent an angel to protect Ken and me, but I had never actually been in the hands of a robber before. Finally we knelt to pray, thanking God for the miracle we had experienced, and committing our lives into his hands.

Alone in my room, I talked to my heavenly Father as I knelt by my bed. "You told me not to be afraid, that I have a Father in heaven who loves me. Oh, Lord, thank You for showing me how You really are caring for me, no matter where I am, especially when I am involved in Your service down here on earth. I will never doubt You!"

The phone rang early the next morning, asking for me. "We have two men whom we have detained and kept under guard all night," a voice said. "Will you please come down to see if you can identify them?"

I couldn't believe it! Was I to face my assailant? When I walked into the room I saw two men sitting there under police guard. Their eyes fastened on me. I looked at them carefully, taking my time, then shook my head. Neither matched what I remembered of the two robbers. I could see the anxiety in their eyes and the relief when I shook my head.

On the way to church, David asked, "How do you

feel about speaking in church?"

"You know, I prayed about this last night," I replied. "If Satan sent that attack to frighten us into running home without accomplishing our goal here, he was mistaken. With God's help, I'll do the best I can."

He smiled. "I'm glad, Alcyon. I think you are right."

The church was filled to capacity again, and sitting on the platform with a row of elders, the pastor, and David, I studied the congregation.

The people seemed to be all dressed in dark colors. Most of the women had their heads covered. But the thing that impressed me the most was the lack of any expression on their faces—no smiles, just all sitting there staring straight ahead. I knew they had gone through more than I could ever imagine. My heart went out to them, and I prayed for words of comfort.

David gave a wonderful talk, and then it was my turn. I just began by saying, "We can't know all that you have gone through behind the iron curtain, but I can see that your faith must have sustained you and brought you here to God's house. We have heard of the tragedy of the orphan children, and we have come to see if we can help." Then I told them about International Children's Care and a story or two of some of the children we had aided.

Soon I saw handkerchiefs coming out, and some began sobbing. Perhaps they had lost children. Certainly they had all suffered loss of some kind. The pastor insisted I stand at the foyer with them to greet the people. Their warm handshakes, hugs, and greetings to me will forever remain in my memory. One old man reached out to take my hand and kissed it.

As we left that day, we all felt rewarded for having met the people. We determined to do what we could to bring comfort, in some way, to the suffering children of Romania.

30 Mama! Mama!

"Mrs. Fleck," Adrian Buconanu called to me while we visited with some English-speaking young people after church. "They have prepared food for you and your friends. Come with me." He led us to a room just off the church patio. Some church women set our food on a table in this small room that was sort of a church kitchen.

It seemed that the Romanian Adventists went to church all day. Many of them brought their lunch and ate in the church patio while waiting for the next meeting to begin at 2:00 p.m. We also attended that meeting. The congregation had assigned someone to translate for us. Another meeting, apparently for a special group, would follow that one.

When we finally climbed the stairs to our room at the hotel, we were ready for a rest. "How did you sleep last night after what happened to you?" Ruthie asked me.

"I'll have to admit that I've had better nights," I responded. "But actually, after thinking about it for a while, I realized that maybe the whole experience was really a blessing."

"What do you mean?" Edna queried.

"You see, in my position as director of children's services, I have to travel a lot, supervising all of the International Children's Care programs for children. Of course that entails a certain amount of risk. I used to be afraid to fly and had to overcome that. There have been other dangerous situations, especially in Guatemala. I have known and felt that God always protects us, but I had never actually been in the hands of the enemy like last night. But as I was reviewing the whole picture in my mind, I realized that I would feel more secure now than before, no matter where I am."

"Why is that, Alcyon?" Ruthie asked.

"Well, last night, right after we were safely back in our room, Ruthie, you said, 'Alcyon, there has been an angel in this room!' "

"I remember."

"You know, I didn't even have time to pray, it all happened so fast. What this all taught me is that our angels are there even before we ask. Actually experiencing that fact, I now realized that I can feel safer than before!"

They both smiled and chorused, "Amen!"

"But I do think we can be more careful and always lock the door immediately!" I added.

"Yes, God expects us to use caution and good judgment," Ruthie advised. "You know, I remember seeing some men sitting in the hall at the foot of the stairs that night."

We stayed on in that room for the remaining time we spent in Romania, but we watched for anyone lingering around in a suspicious way.

On Monday morning another pastor from the union office came to take us to see some more orphanages and buildings. "I've heard about one orphanage at the edge of town that you might like to visit," he said.

"Yes, we need to understand a little of the real situation here about the orphan children. That will make a difference to our board," I replied.

As we traveled, we asked questions. "What do you think brought the big problems for children here in Romania?" I asked.

"First of all," the pastor began to explain, "you have to realize what the conditions were before the recent revolution. The authorities had gradually taken away all of our freedoms. They confiscated property." He directed our attention to rows and rows of nondescript high-rise apartment buildings, all just alike. "There used to be fine old homes there. But the government seized and destroyed them. Then they crowded the working class into those apartments. They were expected to have at least five children. Mothers had to work and leave their children in care centers during the week."

"That would be terribly traumatic for the parents as well as the children," I commented.

"Yes, just imagine!" He sighed, then continued, "I think they found it harder and harder to leave the children, and of course it was difficult on the children themselves. Then the authorities started keeping the children in the orphanage during the week, and sending them home for the weekend."

The rest of our conversation opened our eyes to the trauma that both parents and children suffered.

Eventually, parents abandoned thousands of the children in the orphanages. The human spirit can stand just so much, then the emotions get turned off and people do what they have to do to survive.

Arriving at the orphanage, the pastor spoke to the director, a man, and he offered to show us through the facility. Noticing our dismay at the conditions, he said, "There is never enough money to pay staff to properly care for the children."

The limited help forced them to leave the children in their cribs all day. The staff brought bottles around at certain times and changed diapers on a schedule, but not often enough.

"These children have almost no human contact," Edna remarked.

We saw crib after crib of toddlers, 2 and 3 years old, standing in their cribs, vacant looks in their sad little faces, their heads bobbing back and forth.

At one facility they took us to a back room full of cribs reserved either for handicapped children or babies with AIDS. "Come here and look at this!" I called to Ruthie and Edna. I was standing over a crib of a baby that looked to be a few months old, but was probably older than that. She was hardly more than a skeleton, lying there with her vacant eyes open, flies covering her face.

"Oh, how horrible!" they both exclaimed.

I can never forget the image that stayed with us as we left. Drawn little faces covered with flies, their bodies nothing but bones—it was unbelievable. "There is nothing we can do," the director explained. "We don't get enough money to do better."

Our tour took us to a women's hospital. Actually, the purpose of our visit was possibly for the government to close it and let us use the building. There, too, the building seemed deserted and badly in need of repair. A few patients remained, however, some lying on bare mattresses. A nurse acting as our guide told us that the facility had performed several thousand abortions there each year. "Look in there," I told the others. A woman was lying on a bare mattress in her clothes.

"She is probably waiting for her abortion," the nurse explained.

The woman had turned her face to the wall. My heart ached for her. How would I have coped in a system that forced people to leave their children in the hands of the state and provided no real education or care. I went away from that place of death, sick to my stomach and heart, as I realized how many women had suffered there.

Adrian, our translator, went with me to visit government officials, trying to enlist their cooperation in establishing a facility for children in Romania. At one point he introduced me to a woman, Dr. Lazer, in charge of a children's hospital. She showed us through her hospital and told us of her needs. "We never have enough blankets or diapers or medicines. Especially since the revolution, our budget doesn't begin to cover our needs." We arranged to bring her some of the diapers and blankets we had stored at our warehouse.

Dr. Lazer took a deep interest in our plans for Romania. She arranged for us to meet other officials. Actually, she and I became good friends. Telling us about an unused building still furnished with cribs and other equipment, she went with us and showed us around. Of all the possibilities we saw, this was by far the best.

We looked it over carefully, picturing just how many babies we could care for there. Then I turned to Dr. Lazer. "I think our board will be interested in this, but I need to take them a report. Is there any way we could get a plan or measurements of the building?"

"I'm sure I can arrange that," she told me. Before we left we had a copy of the plans. It seemed as if we had found the answer for our needs.

"Before we can submit a request for the building," both Adrian and Dr. Lazer explained, "you will have to draw up some organizational papers to be recognized by the government."

"Then I should probably get started on that while I am here," I replied. "But I will need some help."

Adrian set up a meeting for the next day, and Dr. Lazer agreed to come and assist us. Although I still needed the ICC board's final approval, they had authorized this trip. We could get the papers all ready. The next day the three of us sat around a table at the Romanian Union office. Among other things, I learned that we had to have an official name in Romanian as well as a local board. It was an interesting discussion. I was eager to choose a name that would give a good idea of what ICC really does.

"Since people here haven't had much to look forward to, how about something such as 'Hope for Children?'" I suggested.

To my surprise, Dr. Lazer reacted quickly. "No! People here don't believe in that word!" It was too soon after the revolution.

Finally we settled on Iubire Si Camin Pentru Copii (Love and Home for Children).

Besides taking a report to our board to get the final approval, we had to raise the needed funds. David Taylor worked with me to present a proposal to Adventist Development and Relief Agency for the initial budget.

The day before we were to leave Romania we went to one more home for children. This orphanage was also an old mansion that the Communists had confiscated. Situated in a large yard surrounded by a fence, it served the 4- to 6-year-old group. Inside, the main room was so full of iron cribs with high sides that you could hardly walk between them. The children were running between the cribs. They immediately surrounded us, reaching up their arms to us and hanging on to our clothes. One little girl begged to be picked up, and Edna took her into her arms. That was a mistake. The child clung to her neck, saying, "Mama, Mama!" When we had to go, the little girl wrapped her arms and legs around Edna, and the caretaker had to forcibly pull her away.

As we walked out the door, a group of children paraded after us into the yard, including Edna's little girl. We walked to the front gate and then along the fence to our car, parked on the side street. The children followed us along the inside of the high chain-link fence. Pleading "Mama! Mama!" they reached out to us through the fence.

As we drove away they continued to call out to us,

their little arms stretched as far as they could through the fence. Tears filled our eyes and our hearts were breaking with that image and their pleas filling our minds.

31 A Place for the Babies

*R*eturning to the International Children's Care office in Vancouver, we found the board enthusiastic about Romania, and Adventist Development and Relief Agency was interested in helping us open a receiving center. First of all we needed to have a contract with the Romanian government for the use of the building that we had located. We chose a director, Marilee Unterseher, who had a master's degree in social work. She found an apartment in Bucharest that could serve as housing for her and as a temporary office. A truckload of clothes and supplies arrived from Western Europe. Everything seemed to be falling in place. But to our great disappointment, we discovered that the post-communist government apparently had no one with the authority to sign a contract. We were back to square one on a building.

Finally, while on another visit to help Marilee find a building, we discussed alternatives. "You know," she began, "maybe I could start visiting desperate families and give out some of these clothes and food that we have stored here until we obtain a building."

"I think that is a good idea," I said. "Let's ask the Romanian Union to tell the pastors what we are doing. Then we can help families that they recommend to us."

She made contact with the churches and soon had a list of families to visit. It was the beginning of our program to help families so they would not have to send their children to an orphanage. Next, Marilee set up the program with a file system to track the families and an accounting system to handle the funds sent from the ICC office. Soon we were assisting 300 families each month with food, bedding, wood for fuel, and even sometimes rent. However, we knew that such a program was really not giving the kind of permanent support that children needed to secure their future. We still wanted to have a receiving center and eventually a children's village. It was not an easy program to run, especially for a single woman.

Eventually Kent and Jan Greve volunteered to go to Romania. Kent had skills in organization and strategic planning, and Jan was a registered nurse. We hoped that they could succeed in making the transition to our regular program of furnishing homes for abandoned children.

They were finally able to rent a house, secure the needed permits to care for children, and we had the beginnings of a receiving center. But the house was too small. Soon it was full of abandoned babies and toddlers brought to us from the children's hospital, and we could accept no more. The next step was to raise money to buy property and to build a permanent receiving center, then the children's village. A friend of Kent's offered to donate $35,000 for the land.

One day he called us. "I think we have a piece of land we can get for the village," he announced. After getting more details, I again went to Romania with high hopes that at last we could obtain our property and provide homes for many children. But soon after I arrived Kent received word the land had a problem involving ownership and thus was not available. We were all terribly disappointed. Kent had hired one of the girls who had helped with the family program to be his assistant. Gabriela, or Gabbi, as they called her, turned out to be a godsend. She knew how to meet officials and get things done. Gabbi, Kent, and Jan met with me the evening after he had received the bad news about the property. "This is the sixth trip I have made to Romania to sign for property," I told them, "and I think it is time to ask God for a miracle. I believe that He wants us here. There is a tremendous need, and that is what ICC is for. I would like for us all to meet tomorrow morning for a special prayer meeting for God's intervention. There have been many miracles for ICC before. Are you willing?"

They were enthusiastic. First we all prayed at home. When we met that morning, we read passages from the Bible in which God tells us to ask and claim His promises. Jeremiah 33:3 declared: "Call unto me, and I will answer thee, and shew thee great and mighty things, which thou knowest not." Another one I had banked on through the years was Jeremiah 32:17: "Ah Lord God! behold, thou hast made the heaven and the earth by thy great power and stretched out arm, and there is nothing too hard for thee."

When we finished praying, I asked, "What do you think our next move should be?"

"There is a piece of land near my village that my parents were assigned for gardens," Gabbi said. "It is about an acre, but is long and narrow, not suitable for building. But there are other lots adjoining. Maybe someone would sell."

It was a weak clue, and we knew we needed lots more land, but it was a place to start. "Let's go look at it."

Heading for the small village of Odobesti, about 30 miles from Bucharest, we stopped to see the piece of land and study the area. After examining it, we agreed that it might work if we could buy more adjoining property.

"Let's go over to my parents house," Gabbi suggested. "My brother has a carpenter shop there. He might know of something."

When we found her brother he did have an idea. "The people who live across the road have some land they want to sell, and it already has buildings on it."

It didn't take Gabbi long to track the clue down. The man wasn't home, but his wife sent someone with us to see the property. A former Communist cooperative farm, it had a nice acreage with three large storage buildings, besides another large building that had been used for offices and more recently for a potato shed. None of the buildings were in good shape, but they were solid, built of cement blocks. We liked the location and it had land surrounding it that might be available. After all our frustrations, this looked like a real possibility. We could envision a receiving center in the best building. "You know we will need a shop and storehouse," Kent mused. "We could use one of the other buildings for that."

Going through the next building, Jan said, "This one could provide office space and rooms for staff and guests."

As we entered the farthest building, we saw it filled with straw at one end. But it too was a solid building, and looking beyond the dirt and holes in the roof, I told them, "I can envision this as a community building with a clinic at one end. In fact, I think there is a chance that Loma Linda might send us volunteer doctors. We could even have certain days when they treated children from the nearby village. Also we could then have a community room where we could hold classes for the village mothers." Our dreaming went on and on.

"How much is it?" we asked the wife.

"You'll have to ask my husband," she answered. "But I can call him on the cell phone."

When she reached him, our hopes plummeted. He wanted $100,000.

Gabbi explained to her that we had only $35,000, so we wouldn't be able to buy it.

"Well, I'll tell him, and he can call you," the woman said.

Since she had her cell phone in her purse, Gabbi gave the woman her number.

We were almost back to Bucharest when Gabbi's phone rang. It was the owner and he soon started coming down a little.

"No. You don't understand," she said as he continued negotiating. "This is an organization that wants to provide homes for children. It is all the money we have."

"We'll have to think about it and get back with you," he concluded. Soon the phone rang again. "We'll let you have it," he announced. Then, "Is it all right if we drive in to see you tonight?"

When Gabbi put the phone down, she almost shouted, "God has heard us. We can have the farm for $35,000!"

True to his word, the owner and his wife came that evening, and we made the deal. After they left, we had another prayer meeting, this time one of praise and rejoicing!

As I write this, we have a beautiful receiving center in Romania with approximately 40 little abandoned babies and children. The court sends them to us, mostly from the children's hospital where their parents, unable to care for them, have abandoned them. One of the big warehouses has already been remodeled and made into an office, guest room, and storage room.

Beyond that, we have just purchased another 25 acres adjoining our property to house the children's village.

My seventh trip to Romania was to attend the dedication of the receiving center along with Donna and Denzil McNeilus. Their generosity had made the remodeling of the center possible. Accompanying them were Pastor and Mrs. Mark Finley. Denzil and Donna were helping the Finleys arrange a citywide evangelistic campaign in Bucharest. But Pastor Finley found time to give our dedication address.

It was an impressive occasion. Many government officials attended, some from the former Communist regime. When the Finleys and McNeilus families arrived, they went straight to the nursery in their tour of the building. Soon I saw Mark Finley in one of the rocking chairs with a baby in his arms. It wasn't long until they had all found a baby to hold. In his address he said, "Back in the nursery I found a beautiful baby to hold." Then he added, "The Bible says that if we do it to one of these little ones, we do it to Jesus. With that baby in my arms, I could imagine holding the baby Jesus, Himself, in my arms." I noticed many in the audience wiping their eyes.

The children we saw in our center are happy and healthy and loved. My thoughts went back to that day we had to leave those little neglected children reaching out through the fence, each calling, "Mama! Mama!"

32 A Call From Thailand

I was home in Battle Ground when the ringing of the telephone woke us out of a sound sleep. It was still dark and I glanced at the clock. Who could be calling at that hour? When I answered, I heard Robert Folkenberg's voice. "Where in the world are you, Bob?" I asked.

"Anita and I are in Bangkok." Before I had a chance to say anything, he went on. "Listen, Alcyon, Anita and I think that International Children's Care should come to Thailand. There is such a need here. We feel so strong about it that we will buy tickets for you and Ken if you will fly here."

He went on to tell of the conditions they had seen and of others they had heard about. "You may not know that Thailand has one of the highest rates of child prostitution in the world," he commented. Of course he had my attention. Then he went on to tell me of the possibilities that he saw, including using some of the land at the mission school in Chaing Mai. "We'll make arrangements for your time here."

We did go to Thailand. Since we had never been in

the Orient before, we found the culture, language, and people very different. But we knew that children are pretty much the same the world over, and children in need exist all around the globe.

Besides the children in Thailand, we learned that hundreds of orphaned children, as well as families, were living in refugee camps along the Thai border with Myanmar, formerly Burma. One of the Adventist pastors had found a group of Adventist Christians in a large camp. They separated to make their own settlement where they could worship and teach their children Christian values. The pastor helped us to send food to these refugees. They established a home for the orphans among them, and we have been able to assist them too.

One of our board members, Paul Edgren, went to Myanmar on a visit. When he visited the mission school he found that the teachers had been taking some of the many orphans into their homes. Paul decided to do something about the situation. The mission had extra land, so he went back home to Redding, California, and raised money to build two homes for children. That was the beginning of ICC in Myanmar.

Once the board made its decision to take ICC to Thailand, money became available to begin constructing cottages. Some of the children brought to us came from conditions of deep poverty, but some were little girls rescued from the prospect of a life of prostitution. We were horrified to learn that even very young girls, 8 to 10 years old, became victims of the wicked trade.

One day as I sat at my desk in the office in Vancouver, a fax came through from Thailand. It read: "We just heard about two very young girls in a tribal village. Someone going through the village offered to take the two girls to Bangkok and give them work. In exchange they would give the parents money to feed their other children. We think that they took the older girl, but the little one ran into the woods. We are hoping we can find her." When such girls reach the city, no one hears from them again. Some get exported to other countries for prostitution, and others wind up in bondage right there in the city. Unfortunately, such incidents are common.

Soon after the first children's house opened, we heard the story of one baby girl. It seems that some of the remote tribes have strange superstitions. One of them demands that if a mother dies in childbirth, the family must bury the baby alive with her. Otherwise, the spirits will bring calamities on the tribe. A teacher walking through a village noticed a funeral going on at the cemetery. As he approached it he realized that a mother had died and that the mourners were in the process of preparing her baby for burial with her. They had placed the infant in a big pot and poured some whiskey in her mouth to make her sleep. The teacher remonstrated with the father, finally persuading him to let him take the baby and find it a home. The child stayed in a pastor's home until they could bring her to the new children's home in Chaing Mai. When we received a picture of this little girl, I wondered, *How many babies that we don't find are suffering that fate?* Seeing the pictures now of our homes in Thailand, bustling with happy boys and girls fills me with gratitude that God helped us to start a program like ICC.

33 The Jesus Truck

We have an appeal from Cambodia," our son, Rick, president of International Children's Care, told us at our regular administrative meeting on a Wednesday morning. "One of the local pastors in Samrung, a city in the north, found a family of children alone. Their mother had just died. It is a strange story. Apparently her husband was killed in the war. Since she and the children were starving, she finally decided that it was better that they all die together so she cooked some poison frogs. Although she ate some, the children didn't like them and refused.

"It seems that the local church property had some empty space. The pastor took it on himself to build a small cottage with lumber he found. He planned to find someone to stay with the children in the cottage. But by the time he was ready to move them in, the baby had died. They are in the house now, and he has a young woman there caring for them. Now he has no money to feed them."

Even though the little rustic cottage didn't fit into our overall plans, we felt that we had to help the pastor.

"He must have a concern for children to do what he did, and he must have a lot of faith," Rick continued.

"Couldn't we make an exception to our policies for new projects and send him some help for food?" I asked. "Then we can see where we go from there."

We did send money for food. In fact, we made arrangements through the local mission to supply funds every month and to begin sponsoring the children. Each month we would learn that the little three-room shack housed more children. The devastating Cambodian civil war had left thousands of children homeless. Soon the little cottage bulged at the seams with 18 children. The yard had a well, but it had never been lined, allowing polluted groundwater to seep into it. We arranged for someone to finish the well. But we knew that something would have to be done soon to provide better living conditions and more room.

Then a call came in the middle of the night to Otis Edwards, formerly the president of the Far Eastern Division of Seventh-day Adventists. Retired, he was serving as assistant to the president of ICC.

It was the last big battle at Samrung between Pol Pot's forces and the national army. Early that morning shots rang out and bedlam broke loose. Smoke from burning houses filled the air and panic spread through the village.

The pastor thought of all those children with only a young woman to protect them. "I've got to get them to the Thai border!" he told his wife. Then hitching a small trailer to his pickup, he drove the safest route he could to the church property. The children were still safe, huddled together in the little cottage with their caretaker.

"Get the children ready to leave." he told the young woman. "Just take the most necessary things. We have to leave immediately."

But just then two of the armed rebels came to the house. The one who seemed to be an officer demanded roughly, "We need your truck. Give us the key!"

Before the pastor could answer, one of the little boys walked right up to the officer and said, "You can't take this truck; it belongs to Jesus!"

The boldness of the child took the man by surprise. "Jesus! Who is he?"

"You don't know who Jesus is?" the boy asked, as if everyone should know Him.

The officer turned to the other soldier. "Do you know who Jesus is?"

"No, but He must be somebody important. Maybe we shouldn't take it." And they hurried away.

All this time the pastor had been praying for help. "Hurry, children! We need to leave!"

And then two more soldiers came, this time from the national army. One of them, also apparently an officer, said urgently but respectfully, "Your car is the only one available in the village. I'm sorry, but we have to take it."

Again the little boy stepped forward. "You can't take this truck. It doesn't belong to us—it belongs to Jesus."

The two soldiers glanced at each other. "Have you heard anything about this man Jesus?" one of them asked the other.

The other soldier looked confused. "No, I haven't heard."

"Every one should know Jesus," the child insisted. "You can't take His truck!"

The officer, nonplused, told the pastor, "I guess we had better not take it then."

As they walked off, the pastor hurried the children and their caretaker into the truck and drove toward the border. A lull in the fighting allowed them to leave town. As he headed down the road with his cargo of 18 children, the pastor thanked God for speaking through a little child and possibly saving all their lives.

That night they crossed the border and located a refugee camp on the other side. It was raining and they had no shelter, but they were safe. The pastor called the mission, telling them what had happened. The mission phoned Otis that night, and he had money wired the next day to purchase tents and food.

As soon as possible the children were taken down through Thailand, back into Cambodia, and then on to the mission in Phnom Penh. The mission provided the children with a rented house until ICC could arrange permanent homes.

We have purchased 25 acres in the center of the country and have already built several homes. The number of children increases as fast as space becomes available. That little boy and the rest of those 18 children now live with houseparents. We are using one of the new homes for a school until we can construct an appropriate building. More and more children are learning about who Jesus is, and about the permanent homes that He is getting ready for them. As I write this report, our country village in Cambodia has 52 children. The houses fill up as fast as we finish them. As I think about the little boy who wasn't afraid to face the soldiers because that truck belonged to Jesus, I thank God that so many children are finding secure homes. But most important of all, they are learning about Jesus, and that changes their lives.

34 The Answer

Christmas was in the air, and the stores had been decked out for the holidays since Thanksgiving. But despite all the festive spirit, there was an undercurrent of concern. The economy was in a slump. The business community was doing everything possible to tempt people to spend their money at the same time charities were sending out letters and flyers. It was the worst time of year for donations to slack off. International Children's Care was feeling the pinch too.

"How are things going with donations this month?" I asked as I entered my son's office. We all realized that we, as well as other nonprofit organizations, depended on December donations to help carry us through the slow months ahead. For ICC, with hundreds of children counting on that monthly income from our main office, it was crucial. Already we could see the red light ahead.

"I'm very concerned," Rick answered. "The slowdown in the economy is showing in the donations the past several months, but especially this month. Here it is, the last week of December. Many of those donors who usually mail a sizable check in December are sending less, if anything at all. And, of course, people with smaller incomes are tightening the belt, not knowing what the future holds."

"Well, if there is one thing we have learned in the past, it is that this is God's program, and our children are His," I said.

"I know. Of course we pray every day for God's blessing on our efforts." Then, after a pause, he continued. "Tomorrow is Thursday, worship day for our staff. I think we will have a special day of prayer for a miracle. There are still a couple days when we can get donations with this year's postmark for tax purposes. God could impress a number of people to send more than they had planned."

"I'm glad you are thinking that way," I responded. "Sometimes it seems that we need to be reminded that everything we have done in the past is because of God's special blessing."

The next morning, with all the staff gathered upstairs in our assembly room, Rick got out his guitar as usual, and we began to sing. Different ones requested their favorites, and then we sang one of our theme songs: "The Family of God." That song is special for ICC. We want all of our children around the world to know that they are part of God's family. When we began the verse that starts out, "At the door of an orphanage—," I just prayed silently, *Lord, You know about all of our children, Your little orphans. Please give us a special blessing today.*

After the reading of several biblical promises and

the regular announcements, Rick began, "You all know about the economic crisis this year, and some may realize what an impact it has had on us. Through the years we have prayed for many things, and God has helped us through every crisis. Today we are going to have a special day of prayer. The lives and welfare of hundreds of children in our projects around the world depend on us here. I would like for us to break up in small groups and pray earnestly that God will provide the funds that we need to keep this program for children afloat. We are actually $50,000 short of where we should be right now to meet the budgets in the coming slow months."

The people who work in ICC, as Christians, have a special interest in helping children. The murmur of prayers filled the room. When we rose from our knees it was time to go to our different offices for the day's work.

The next day, Friday, and our last day in the office before the new year, Rick and Ken were both in my office discussing some problem. Lori, the secretary, stuck her head through the door. "I just had a call from some lady in Arizona. She said she is sending a check for $50,000, and she wants to be sure that it is dated for this year. I asked her if she said $50,000, and she answered, 'Yes, I hope you can use it.'" Lori's face beamed with a big smile. She had been there when we prayed for $50,000.

The little committee we had been having instantly turned into a prayer and praise committee!

On our first day in the office after New Year's Day the mail included a letter from Arizona. The individual had never sent money before. When we opened the envelope, the check was there—$50,000! After letting all of our staff know of the miracle God had given us, I went to my office and dialed the number of the sender of the check. A young woman answered.

"I just wanted to call to thank you for your generous check that just arrived. You need to know that your check was a direct answer to prayer," I said, then explained the situation.

"Don't thank me," she replied. "Thank God. I received a windfall and prayed for guidance as to what I should do with it. I felt impressed to send this to you."

After I hung up I sat at my desk, thinking of all that God had done for us in ICC. I remembered that day in the woods when I struggled with the decision about accepting the request to direct a new orphanage program. And I remembered the quotation I read. "When we give ourselves wholly to God, and in our work follow His directions, He makes Himself responsible for its accomplishment."

Bowing my head, I prayed, "Thank You, Lord, for reaffirming my faith. I know that Your promises never fail!"

35 Children Can Preach

We had planned the Rancho, a structure built of poles with a palm leaf roof to provide shade and protection from the rain, to serve as a shelter for picnics in the middle of the park area at The Pines. The children's homes surround the park, each on the outside edge of the road and facing the park. The local mission had built a church at the secondary school. But as the number of the homes increased, we needed a church of our own. The director and the children decided to make the Rancho into their church. They made a platform at the front, and the carpentry shop provided rustic pews. Pine trees and hibiscus bushes surrounded the shelter. The birds could flit through the building, and cool breezes made it pleasant.

We began to call it the children's church. Although houseparents, teachers, and directors did attend it, they were the counselors, and we encouraged the children to take an active part according to their ages. Those who were older and had been baptized served as junior elders, deacons, and deaconesses. An older child usually acted as the director of Sabbath school and others taught the classes.

One Friday night I sat in the Rancho after arriving that day from Guatemala City. The generator was turned on so there was sufficient light from bulbs hanging from the rafters. Since the children had known I was coming, they had decorated the Rancho with pine needles on the floor, giving it a wonderful aroma. They flocked around me for hugs and kisses and then followed me in. Those who got there first were now sitting beside me and others crowded onto the same bench.

One of the teenage girls was leading the song service. After a boy offered the opening prayer a group of small children marched up and sang the special music.

I knew that the children's church offered various classes. One trained those who wanted to participate in evangelistic activities. Most of the children could not wait to attend the baptismal class. But the preacher's class especially intrigued me. It surprised me how many children wanted to learn to preach—even the girls.

The orphanage director took groups to nearby villages, where the children visited the homes. They offered free Bible lessons that they would bring week by week and then pick up as the people filled the lessons out. The pastor took the older children to different villages to hold evangelistic meetings. Again the children had an active part. In one village they established a congregation and then helped to build, block by block, a church to house them.

When they announced the speaker this Friday night, someone had to bring a stool. The boy who was going to present the message wasn't tall enough to be seen over the pulpit. I listened closely as he spoke, and was amazed at his delivery and depth of thought. He spoke on the sacrifice of Jesus on the cross. I can say that I had never heard that subject presented in a way that touched my heart more. The pastor was sitting beside me in the audience. I knew that the boy, not more than 11 or 12, had gone to the preacher's class.

The audience was very attentive. At the end of his talk the boy made a call. The pastor leaned over to me and whispered, "I didn't know he was going to do this!"

"I'm sure there are many here tonight who would like to come forward to express your gratitude for what Jesus did there on that cross for us," the child said in a respectful and sincere way. "If you do, just come down here to the front so I can pray with you." Many of the children reverently went forward.

Later, the pastor went to the front and said to everybody, "I think that Mommy Fleck would like to hear about your missionary work. Who would like to tell what you are doing?"

One little boy, about 10 or 11, walked right up. "Oscar and I—Oscar was my partner," he began, "we went up to a house where we had left Bible lessons before. There was a big dog in the yard, and we were afraid of him, but we got up to the door. The lady invited us in. There was an old, old man there too. The lady began to tell us her problems. We gave her counsel as best we could. Then we asked her if she would like for us to pray with her, and she said yes. So we knelt down, and it was my turn to pray. So I started to pray, but the old man started to pray too. I didn't know what to do, so I just began to pray louder, but he prayed louder too, and then I prayed louder, and finally I won!" Although there were smiles in the audience, the boy was not trying to be humorous.

It is always interesting to note how fearless the children are when they take part in any public meeting. Even the smallest ones will march right up to sing or recite a poem. When we call this a children's church, it really is just that. They are the ones who clean and decorate the church, and they fill major roles in the services. It is understandable that many of them aspire to be pastors or teachers when they grow up.

Some time later the pastor told me a story about some meetings the children helped him with. "We went to a village on Sabbath afternoon to invite the people out for the next Sunday evening. Two of the teen girls went together to one part of the village. When they knocked on a door, a woman came to the door crying. 'Why are you crying?' they asked.

"'Because my children are all very sick, and I have no money for a doctor,' she explained.

"One of the girls told the woman, 'Do you know that Jesus can make your children well?'

"'No, I didn't know that,' she answered.

"'If you would like, we will pray for your children,' the other girl offered.

"'Oh, please do!' And the girls knelt down and prayed for the sick children.

"The mother and her children were all at the meeting the next night," the pastor concluded.

Back at the trailer where I stayed, I walked out on the patio situated on a little rise. The generator had been turned off, and my gas lantern lit the trailer. The stars filling the sky seemed so bright they appeared to hover just out of reach. Out there, away from other lights, the nights are spectacular. I could look down across the park with the candlelights twinkling in the windows of the homes. Then one by one the lights went out and our campus was quiet except for the night sounds of frogs, crickets, and some birds. These children, in all of these homes, were there because God had helped us to find and rescue them. Now they were learning about a God they can trust. And they were discovering that their Father in heaven has a plan for each of them.

36 Julia and Javier

*B*y the time Ken and I arrived at the Portland airport that morning, Marilyn and Dan Patchin were already there. "I don't see Mary Lou yet or Sarah," I remarked, studying the line of people waiting to check in. Mary Lou Ham had been a donor to International Children's Care for some time, and this trip to actually see the children she had helped through the years was a dream come true.

"There's Sarah," my husband said, glancing toward the door. She had been adopted from The Pines years before. "And, yes, Mary Lou is just coming in, too."

"I guess we are all here now!" I said as we all got in line. "This will be the great adventure!"

We were on our way to Guatemala to attend the wedding of Julia, the first wedding at The Pines for one of our children. She was marrying Javier, a theology student from the university in Costa Rica. From there we were going up into the mountains where Salvador (I tell his story in my book, *Child of the Crossfire*) and Sarah had been born.

Marilyn Patchin was one of our charter board members for International Children's Care. At the beginning, when only a handful had to do everything, she supervised our warehouse and the preparation of shipping containers to our first project. She would gather some of her friends to sort clothing and pack boxes and then load them onto the truck. For years Marilyn volunteered her time and effort for that responsibility. But she had never visited any of our projects. Often, as she held up some of the cute little dresses, she would say, "I wish I could be there and see which little girl will wear this." And then she and her husband, Dan, adopted our first baby. Now that he had retired from his medical practice, they were free to travel.

Sarah was Ruthie in *Child of the Crossfire.* Those who have read it will remember that she was the baby aboard the helicopter along with Salvador, Rosie, and several others. The general who brought her to us said that she had been found in a cave after a battle with the guerrillas. The military supposed her mother had hidden her there and then been killed.

But after Salvador went back and found that his mother was still alive, "Ruthie's" parents came to ask him if he had seen a tiny girl. Since she was his cousin, he remembered her, and knew she was in the United States. When I phoned her to let her know that we had found her birth parents, she cried for joy. From then on her dream was to go to Guatemala and visit them.

When Salvador visited us after graduating from college, Sarah came, too. We took her with us to meet his plane. It was quite a reunion after all those years since she had left the country as a little girl. Salvador became the big brother she had never had. "Mommy Fleck, if you go to Guatemala, may I go with you?" she had asked me. Now her aunt had given her a ticket, and she was on her way. She would travel with us to The Pines, then accompany us up into the mountains to see her birth parents.

The Patchins and Mary Lou had read *Child of the Crossfire* and also met Salvador when he had visited the United States. We were all eager to see the remote area where that incredible story had taken place and meet his and Sarah's families.

Arriving in Guatemala City, Maria Feldmann, our director at the receiving center, met us at the airport with the van we have there. The next morning the group toured the facility. In the first room is the nursery. Bending over one crib, I asked Maria, "Is this your youngest baby? It is so tiny."

"Yes," she answered. "This little fellow came in just this week. The police brought him to us in the middle of the night."

The others came to look. "Where did the police get him?" they asked.

"Most of the children we get are found on the streets, but sometimes it is a case of child abuse that someone reports," Maria explained.

"Poor babies!" Mary Lou said, shaking her head. It wasn't long before both she and Marilyn each had one in their arms.

Toddlers swarmed the wide hall and the adjoining playroom. Soon Dan was carrying around a little fellow who had tugged at his pant leg. All the children like to see visitors.

I explained to the group how we had found this building, which had been a psychiatric clinic. On the flat roof we had added a big laundry area, extra room for staff, and a fenced-in play space.

As we were touring the building, Maria asked Dr. Patchin if he would look at a sick baby. While we have a visiting local doctor, she wanted another opinion. Soon Dan was in our little clinic room, examining several children.

The next day we loaded up the van and headed to Poptun, the nearest village to The Pines, a 250 mile trip from Guatemala City. When Juana heard that we were coming, she was concerned. "Bandits have attacked a number of people on the road to Poptun," she warned us. From there it was seven miles through the jungle to The Pines. "Some of the teachers from our secondary school have been held up and robbed." Since it was a terrible road, with deep ruts, cars had to creep along, making them vulnerable to bandits.

"What do you think, Juana? Is it safe for us to bring visitors?"

"Beto and I will work on it. I think we can get some help from the local police if you come."

Ken and I did considerable thinking and inquiring as to whether we should bring a load of Americans over that road. But Juana and her husband, Beto, assured us they had made arrangements to have a guard go with us. We were to meet them at a gas station just before reaching Poptun at 4:00 p.m. that afternoon. No one wanted to travel that road after dark, and the sun goes down around 6:00 p.m. in that part of the world.

While still on the main highway to the east coast from Guatemala City we encountered a terrible wreck that completely blocked the road for several hours. A truck and a loaded bus had collided. When we finally got past it, we knew we would have to avoid any unnecessary stops. Maria had fixed us a lunch, so we just passed sandwiches and food around as we road along. Ken and Dan took turns driving.

Finally, just before 4:00 we arrived at the gas station, but Juana and Beto weren't there yet. "Why don't we drive on through the village so you can see what Poptun looks like?" Ken suggested.

When we returned to the gas station, we noticed a school bus there. Getting closer we saw that it was our bus from The Pines, full of children. They had come to escort us through the jungle. Other staff members had accompanied them in their cars.

The children all piled out of the bus, running up to Ken and me. "Mommy and Poppy Fleck!" they chorused. And then someone unrolled a banner with "Welcome" printed in huge letters. They greeted our visitors with hugs and kisses, too. Then the children all lined up and began to sing. They gave us a short program right there at the station. When the procession was ready to start, with our car in the middle, the children shouted, "Mommy Fleck! Come and ride with us!" So I climbed in the front seat of the bus. Soon two of the smallest girls were on my lap, and others crowded in to sit by me. As we started down the road, Juana, who was sitting nearby, pointed to a car parked on a side road. "See that car? That is the police. He is going ahead of us to clear the road, and he will be nearby if we need him."

It was a long ride over those seven miles of jungle. The ruts were deep and sometimes full of water. All the way to The Pines the children sang. As soon as one song ended, another child would start another song, and the rest all joined in. Our bus lumbered along, inching its way over the narrow road, with the jungle crowding in on both sides. We were thankful to know the police was nearby and that other cars were in front and behind us. Bandits would have had a problem!

When we neared our gate, the bus stopped and someone opened the gate. Suddenly, firecrackers of every kind and size exploded. All the other children, along with their little band of drums, were there to welcome us. They beat the drums and shouted. It was a first class welcome!

The guest house was ready for the visitors. It had been built and furnished by the McNeilus family. Ken and I stayed in the RV trailer that served as our home there. Juana soon called us to her house to eat. Everyone who has ever been there knows what a spread she puts on.

Preparations were in full swing for the wedding. Julia was at Juana's house, putting the last touches on her veil. Javier, the groom, had arrived with his family. I had already met him. In fact, when they first began to date seriously at Central American Adventist University in Costa Rica, I was there visiting. One of our board members, Alice Schultz, had made it possible to have an ICC house near the university for our children who want to go on to college. The girls lived there, and the boys resided in the dorm but came there to eat.

One day Javier stopped by to see me. "May I speak with you in private?" he said. We went into the living room, and he immediately came to the point. "Mommy Fleck, since Julia doesn't have parents, I want to ask you for permission to marry her. I am going to be a minister, and Julia is my dream of a minister's wife."

We talked about their plans and a little about him and his family. I was happy to give him permission to marry Julia. And I was thrilled that this little girl who had come to us so many years before had chosen a man like Javier to be her husband.

Ken would officiate at the wedding, which would take place right there in the Rancho, and Julia had asked me to walk up with her. Since Javier and Salvador had been part of the official university quartet, they had become best friends. Salvador would sing at the wedding and be a groomsman.

It was our first wedding at The Pines. Julia had insisted that she be married in the Rancho, and Javier's family all had to travel from Honduras to be there. It is interesting that every one of ICC's older children, who have talked to me about it, declare that they will be married at The Pines! But after all, that is their home and they have a deep love for that place.

Juana was surprised to see Sarah, whom she remembered as little Ruthie. They hugged each other and cried together. Then, when we went to eat at Juana's house, one of our former housemothers was there, visiting and helping Juana. It happened to be the woman who for many years had been one of our best housemothers, and the one that Sarah remembered as her mother. Sarah just flew into her arms and cried and cried. It indicated how much love exists in that place for the children.

The wedding was beautiful and especially meaningful for me. I know my eyes were glistening as I remembered Julia when she first came, at age 8, after her mother died. The girl had been one of our first children in the orphanage.

Things had greatly changed during the years. Instead of one house full of children with an untamed forest behind it, we now had a seven-teacher primary school and 12 homes full of children surrounding the Rancho. The ICC now operates the nearby mission academy, renovated and serving approximately 300 students from all over Guatemala, including our own young people. The forest is now a beautiful campus with flowers and trees lining the paths leading from the homes to the church in the middle.

The 20 years that Ken and I had given to ICC (even though difficult and often trying our faith and strength) had been some of the best, most fulfilling years of our lives. Looking at all those beautiful children in the audience, and those at the altar, I could say with all my heart, "It was worth it! A thousand times yes!"

37 Salvador's Mountains

Since Salvador's home was in the mountains on the other side of the country, we would have to return to Guatemala City. Salvador went on ahead of us to his mother's house to help prepare for our visit. "There is a little hotel in the village, and I will arrange for you to stay there," he told us. When we arrived back at the receiving center, he phoned to let us know that he had everything arranged, and we told him the approximate time of our arrival.

Maria would accompany us. Later we learned how lucky we would be to have her along. It would be an all-day trip, counting the time we planned to spend in Chichicastenango on the way. Maria packed a box of food, part of it for the trip, and part as a supplement that we might need in the village. Since Salvador's village is in the mountains at an altitude of more than 6,000 feet, we knew it would be cold. It was December and cold even in Guatemala City, so we all took the warmest clothing we had, and Maria stacked extra blankets in the car.

Sarah had brought some extra money to get Christmas presents for her family. She did most of that shopping in Chichicastenango, a typical Indian village on our way. Salvador had told us of the extreme poverty we would see. We learned that the foreign guerrilla leaders in the civil war had actually made their head-quarters in Salvador's mountains. His village, the last large one on the road, had taken the brunt of the violence. A third of the population had lost their lives. When the conflict finally ended, it left the people with heavy property damage and a poverty that, 17 years later, they still had not recovered from. Because Sarah understood that her family was extremely poor, she tried to buy practical things. Although she didn't have a lot of money, she brought her mother a beautiful set of drinking glasses. The truth is the woman had never owned any before.

Chichicastenango is a typical Mayan village. When Ken and I used to go there it was still just an Indian village, much as it had been for centuries. But now the main plaza was full of food and souvenir booths, and tourists filled all the streets. However, that seemed to be about as far as most tourists go. As we proceeded toward the mountains, we left modern civilization behind.

"Did we stay in Chichi too long?" I asked as Ken drove along. "Are we going to make it before dark?" We knew that the danger of robbers increased the further we got into the hills.

"Well, I don't think we had better be lingering or stopping any more than necessary," he replied.

Soon we left the asphalt roads behind and began to climb. The road had countless steep, narrow, and sharp curves. Sometimes we wondered what we would do if we met a car. The scenery was out of this world, though, and the road itself was almost out of this world too! We wondered how soon we would see Salvador's village in the distance, but we went on and on. Then it began to get dark and we still weren't there. Finally, we came to a rather sizable village and stopped for gas. My husband asked how much farther to our village. "You should make it in another hour," the attendant replied.

The road had been getting worse and worse. Ken had had to drive so slowly that we wondered if we would ever get there. It wasn't a happy thought to be on such a road if we should encounter bandits.

Dan and Marilyn asked if we might find some kind of a pension or hotel in the village, and then go on in the morning. Ken turned to the man at the station. "Have there been any bandit attacks lately?"

"Not for a week or two," he answered matter-of-factly.

When my husband got back in the car, he said, "Let's have a vote as to whether we go on or try to stay here." He realized that our passengers were getting worried.

"What do you think?" I said to him.

"I've been thinking and praying," he answered slowly. "The man at the gas station says the road is better from here on. Salvador and his family will be waiting for us and may get alarmed if we don't show up. Also, we don't know how difficult it might be to find room for all of us here. I guess I would favor going on, but we'll do what the majority decides."

Someone in the back seat asked, "Alcyon, what is your vote?"

I thought for a while, then said, "I guess I would trust Ken's judgment."

"OK, let's go!" Dan almost shouted, and the rest chorused, "Yes, let's go!"

"Before we start, let's have a prayer," Ken suggested. "Why don't you pray, Dan?" We were all praying silently as Dan asked God to send angels along with us. Then we were on our way. It was true that the road did improve a lot.

Maria, always an optimist, suggested, "Let's sing Christmas Carols!"

From then until we drove into the village we sang with all our hearts. I know we were all praying, too. Salvador's village had only one hotel, and we stopped in front of it. When Maria went in to look, she came out laughing. We wondered why. She was curious how a bunch of Americans would react when they saw their rooms. By then we were all ready to be good sports, no matter what we found. Actually, when we saw the way the people were living, we realized what a good place we had. However, Ken and I, even though old-time missionaries, admitted that we had never felt so far from civilization.

Salvador had gone to call the Guatemala City receiving center to find out when we had left, but he returned soon after we arrived. His mother lived just up the cobblestone street. As soon as we found our rooms and unloaded, he announced, "They're holding supper for you," and took us to his mother's home. We hadn't realized that Sarah's family would be there, but Salvador told us they were waiting too. I noticed that the girl became very quiet as we drove up the street. Salvador went in first. Before we had even gotten out of the car, we could hear Sarah's mother crying inside—actually, she was wailing. It seemed as if the grief from all the years when she had wondered what happened to her baby now suddenly poured out.

After we all got out, Sarah remained in the back seat, pale and unable to move. Salvador climbed back in the car, put his arm around her, and said, "Come on, Sarah. I'll stay right with you. Don't be afraid." The event she had longed for, and come so far for, suddenly seemed to overwhelm her. Finally, when Salvador almost pulled her out, she seemed to get hold of herself. With a smile she went in to meet the people who had given her life.

The only light came from a dim bulb at the end of a cord hanging in the middle of the room, but it revealed a room full of people. They included other members of Salvador's family as well as neighbors and friends. It was something that the village would talk about for years. After all, they had all suffered tremendous losses too. But their loved ones had never come back. Now it was as if someone had appeared from the dead.

Sarah's little mother just took her into her arms and moaned and cried, talking in her native dialect about all that she had suffered. When she finally let her go, the father, a tall man, took the girl into his arms, weeping, caressing her face and hair. I can tell you there was not a dry eye in the crowd. When I remember that moment, the tears still come. I learned again that those suffering around the world, no matter where or how humble the people may be, have feelings just as deep as ours.

Sarah's mother kept saying, "I didn't mean to let you out of my sight. I am so sorry I lost you!" Later, we learned the story behind that statement.

Finally the tears ceased. Sarah sat at one side between her mother and father who kept looking at her and touching her. The room was full of people, all of them in their typical Indian dress. Sarah's mother was nursing a baby, maybe 8 or 9 months old, and pregnant with another one. The girl soon learned the names of all the brothers and sisters born after she left. She had two older brothers, but only one was home. It was touching to see the love he had for her. He remembered that day when, in their flight from the soldiers, she had disappeared. Guerrillas had taken over the village, and the army had suspected everyone of them as its enemy.

The food Salvador's family gave us had been cooked on an open fire on the ground in a lean-to kitchen in the back. They served us the best they had, which was very little. Salvador's mother had not yet returned from a nearby village, but his sisters and other family members were there. The rest of that evening they spent telling us about their families and learning from us how we happened to have their children. Since the majority spoke only an Indian dialect, someone had to translate everything, first into Spanish and then into English for our visitors. Before we left for our hotel, they told us that the Protestant church across the street was available to us, so we arranged to have a service on Sabbath.

Our hotel could be counted as part of a missionary adventure. The rooms were in a daylight basement. Some rooms had no windows, and those that did, had broken glass that let in the bitter cold air. We put on all the blankets that Maria had brought, and even then some of us huddled there wishing for morning to come. *How can these people exist?* I kept wondering. *Their houses have no heat, except the little fires they make on the dirt floors in the middle of the room. They have very little bedding and just simply roll up in the blankets they have.* We didn't spend much time the next morning in the cold showers.

Maria asked the woman who ran the hotel if she could cook on her stove, so Maria did provide us with some hot food. We were all thankful for the fruit, crackers, cheese, and other supplies that she had thought to bring. Then Maria took the dishes upstairs to the woman's kitchen to wash.

The next day Sarah's parents wanted us to eat at their house. It was a smaller place than the house belonging to Salvador's mother. Sarah's grandfather was there, an old man who had gone through the harrowing days when their village was a battlefield. His wife had died soon after. He loved Sarah just as any grandfather would. Almost as soon as we arrived, Sarah's mother gave her a hand-woven skirt, blouse, and headpiece just like her own and that of all the other woman in the village. She took her daughter next door to the grandfather's house and helped her to change into the costume. When they returned, the mother was happy and beaming and everyone clapped. Sarah did look beautiful. Now it seemed to her mother that the girl really belonged to them. Salvador must have told them we were vegetarians because we saw a whole uncooked, skinned chicken that was to have been our dinner hanging on the wall near the ceiling.

It was interesting to observe the difference between Sarah and her siblings. She was taller, with a glow of health that they didn't have. They lived on a diet that allowed them only to exist and little else.

The church service on Sabbath was interesting. Most of the family was there as well as some neighbors. Salvador's mother sat on the front row and glowed with pride. I'm sure it was the first time she had heard him preach. While she doesn't understand his faith yet, she is open. Because she can't read, it will take her a while to learn what he believes. Already she has said how happy she is that he was raised by Christians. Salvador commented to me that he thought that our meeting there was the first Seventh-day Adventist service ever held in that village. His desire is to go back to his village as often as possible and bring them the message of salvation that he loves.

On our last night there we gathered again in Salvador's home and heard more of their story. One of his cousins, who had gone away to become a lawyer, was present and told us of his memories as a child. He said he remembers coming out of his house in the morning as a little boy to see dead bodies on the street. The conflict affected every family. The villagers found themselves hostage between the guerrillas and the army. Either side would kill those it considered traitors.

Sarah's mother looked sad because she assumed that her daughter would be immediately leaving with us. When I told her that Sarah would be staying a week more before returning to Guatemala City with

Salvador, her expression changed completely. She just smiled all over.

We found that the entire family were Christians and serving God the best they knew. The simple kindness and love they constantly expressed especially impressed me. We can never know where all of God's children are around the world.

Before we left that night I asked Salvador if his mother still remembered the song she had always sung to him as a child (it appears in the book, *Child of the Crossfire*). He asked her in her dialect, and she nodded.

"Would you sing it for us?" I asked.

When he translated my request she began. In her untrained, but plaintive and clear voice, she began to sing. Salvador sat by her side. As she sang, he put his arm around her, leaning his head on her and crying. Soon we were all crying. Later, as we went to the hotel, I saw that Marilyn was crying, her heart breaking for these people who have suffered so much.

38 The Love of His Life

*J*ulia and Salvador had both graduated the month before at Central American Adventist University in Costa Rica. Julia now had a degree in business administration and Salvador one in theology. After returning from the trip to his village, he talked to me about his future plans.

"There are several openings for me, and I am praying that God will show me in a definite way just where he wants me," he said. "My desire is to follow His leading and go where I can lead many people to know Jesus and love Him like I do." Then, after a pause, he began to tell me more. "You know, Mommy Fleck, I have come to understand something important. Remember at the time of the massacre? As I think back, I realize that I didn't have to walk into the hands of the army. I really believe that God blinded my eyes. He had to let me be captured to get me to where He wanted me, the place where I could learn to know Him and His plan for my life."

I had been sure for a long time that the boy had come to us for a purpose. God must have had His hand over him since he was a child. It is an awesome thought for me to realize God's timing, even to placing International Children's Care out there in the jungle, right next door to the army base just before the civil war started.

"So which of the openings do you think you will take, Salvador?"

"I've prayed a lot. I wanted to go to the mission that is in charge of the area that includes my village. But perhaps I need more experience first, so I have decided to answer the first official call I get."

"I think that is a good decision," I told him.

Not long after we returned home, Salvador phoned us. "The president of the East Mission of Guatemala just contacted me," he announced. "They have voted for me to pastor a district near Jalapa and want me to come by the office on Tuesday. The district has 14 groups and three churches. The pastor in the next district can give me advice when I need it. Mommy Fleck, I believe this call is from God, and I have accepted it."

"I believe it too, Salvador. We will be praying for you."

For a few weeks we didn't hear anything from him. His new district was up in the hills, and he traveled from village to village. Even though he had a room in someone's home, he was seldom there. He was like an itinerant preacher, staying with the people wherever he went. Soon we heard that he was preparing many for baptism. He was tireless in his efforts.

An active layman in Jalapa loved to be involved in evangelism. He had been a Nazarene pastor before learning about the Sabbath and other Seventh-day Adventist doctrines. Since he was from a Mayan village, he was fluent in both Spanish and the native dialect and spent much time translating the Bible into his dialect. When he became acquainted with Salvador, he saw the young man's dedication and zeal and offered to work with him. Together, they gave Bible studies and conducted evangelistic and other meetings.

Salvador had had several different girlfriends during his years at the university. He knew in his heart that he wanted a wife with the same missionary spirit he had, and he had prayed that God would lead him to the right girl. During his senior year the professors encouraged the ministerial students to pray for the right wife before leaving school since they would have more choices on campus. For a while he did think he had found the right one. However, as time went on, he realized that the girl, who was taking nursing, was very focused on her medical career. It was a painful decision, but he started his ministry single.

Soon he realized that a young single minister can be the object of attention not only for the young women in the church, but also their mothers! But he was still praying for the one that would fit into God's plan. As he visited the home of his new helper he discovered that the layman had a daughter. Bilingual, Mayra was the secretary at an Adventist school of about 300 children. Salvador noticed that she never had a male escort, and he liked her looks. But mostly, he saw what an interest she took in her father's evangelistic activities. She was friendly, but in a distant way. Finally, he asked someone about her.

"She is a wonderful Christian girl," a friend said,

"but people say that she doesn't ever plan to marry. She won't date anyone."

Salvador still wanted to get acquainted with her. Finally, one night he came to see her father, but the man hadn't arrived home yet. While he waited, Mayra tried to make polite conversation. Eventually Salvador got the courage to inquire why she didn't plan to marry. "Would you ever marry a minister?" he asked.

"Yes," she answered softly.

Salvador's heart leaped. *Could this be the girl God was saving for him?*

He realized that Mayra was a serious young woman, and that he needed to plan carefully how to learn to know her better. But with the conviction that God was leading him, he began to pursue his purpose. When he invited her to help with the meetings, he discovered that she was especially talented in working with children. She loved to assist in the children's Sabbath school, and she was an excellent storyteller.

Unknown to Salvador, Mayra had a reason for her decision not to marry. Several years before she had attended a youth rally that touched her heart in a special way. Although she was already baptized and active in the church, at that meeting she became convinced that God had a special place for her, and that it was to be as a pastor's wife. She made a vow to God that she would keep herself for the pastor that God had in mind for her.

When she reached college age she desperately wanted to go to Costa Rica, but her family had no funds for that. Finally, she decided to attend the local college, take a secretarial program, and leave it up to God to find her a pastor husband. She finished her course and then went to work at the school. Although she loved children, she had resigned herself to working for God even if she didn't have a chance to get married. There were no single pastors around. No one, not even her parents, knew of the resolve in her heart.

When Salvador asked her his question, she didn't take it as a proposal, but her heart leaped. She was still determined to be sure that God was leading. After all, Salvador hadn't said, "Would you marry me?" She had prayed for a pastor husband, but she didn't expect an answer as good as this. This young man had every qualification to make him among the most promising of young ministers. He was handsome, had a wonderful way with people, was a good preacher, and a beautiful singer. She knew that the eyes of all the single girls were on him even though he hadn't gone with any of them. Why would he choose her when she hadn't even made herself available? In the privacy of her room, she knelt to pray. "Oh, dear Father in heaven! Could this possibly be the answer?"

Meantime, Salvador was doing some serious thinking and praying of his own. He had prayed for the right wife, but he had not expected the strange stirring he felt in his heart! Somehow he had to see more of Mayra.

Although his work was extremely demanding, Salvador spent as much time with her as he could. On weekends she came to the meetings with her father. In accord with traditional custom, before he would seriously date her, he talked to her father. "Don Alfonso, [the "Don" is a respectful term to use when addressing a man by his first name], I think you must know I am interested in your daughter, and I want you to know that my intentions are serious. May I have your permission to date her seriously?"

Alfonso smiled. "Salvador, from what I have seen of you so far, I am happy to speak for my wife and me to give you permission to court my daughter."

Salvador breathed a sigh of relief, then reached for the man's hand. "You can count on me to treat your daughter with respect. Thank you for your confidence in me."

Then one day I had a phone call from Salvador. Since I hadn't heard from him for quite a while, I was eager to know how he was doing. "How are things going in your work, Salvador?"

"Everything is going great, Mommy Fleck. We are having another baptism this Sabbath." Then he paused before continuing. "I wanted to tell you about someone. Her name is Mayra." Then he went on to tell all about her and her wonderful qualities.

Of course I had to give some advice. "Just take enough time to really know her, and pray a lot about it."

It was several months before he contacted us again. But we heard much about him. Reports came to us of what he was doing for his churches. Juana told me that someone from that area described to her this young man who was winning many people for God, and how well everyone liked him. We continued to pray for Salvador.

39 The Wedding

Now that Mayra's parents had given their approval, Salvador could visit her officially. She went along to the meetings as often as she could, and their friendship grew. Mayra had never been in love before, but now she was sure that she was falling in love.

Salvador had so many groups and churches to care for, besides the evangelistic meetings and the new converts to study with, that he didn't have as much time to spend with Mayra as he wanted. But wherever he was, she was in the back of his mind. *What would it be like to have a girl like Mayra to help me in my work, to pray with me, and, yes, to be the mother of my children?* More and more the conviction deepened. He had no doubt that she was the one. As soon as it seemed appropriate, he would ask her to marry him.

He had told Mayra and her family so much about The Pines where he had grown up that they longed to visit it. Finally, Salvador called Juana. "I think you know that I have a *novia* [girlfriend] here in Jalapa. Her father is a lay evangelist and works with me. They know

I am serious about her and they want to see The Pines. I'm going to come with them this next week, if it is all right with you."

Of course, Juana told him to bring Alfonso and his wife (Mayra could not accompany them because of her duties at the school). Salvador showed them all around the place, including the house where he grew up. They visited the secondary school where he had studied before going to Costa Rica. Not only were they deeply interested in learning what International Children's Care was doing for the abandoned children in Guatemala, they also wanted to know how The Pines had prepared a young man with Salvador's special qualities.

Since Juana realized that people of Jalapa were more sophisticated than in some areas of Guatemala, she was concerned that Salvador's future wife understand his real origin. She determined to discuss it with them. Juana herself is a Mayan Indian and understood that prejudice sometimes does exist toward the Mayan Indians. Like any mother she was looking out for any possible problems in Salvador's future. "Has Salvador told you about his family and his village?" she asked Mayra's father. "Do you realize that most of them don't speak Spanish?"

Alfonso smiled and replied, "Don't worry about that, Señora. You may not know that my mother wears the typical dress. I myself, speak a dialect since I came from Coban." That is an area known to be part of Indian country.

Juana now realized that Mayra and Salvador had similar backgrounds, a fact that would make for better family relationships. She knew that although Salvador had grown up in a different environment than his mother's village and no longer lived like the people in his village, he was fiercely loyal to his mother and her culture.

"Mayra, would you like to visit my mother and family?" he said one day. "I've told you all about them, but I would like to take you there. I want my mother to know you. Of course I would invite your parents to go with us." Salvador eagerly awaited her reaction to his suggestion.

"I would love to meet your family, Salvador, especially your mother. From what you have told me she must be a special person."

By now they had been dating for some time. Every day he felt more and more sure that Mayra really was the love of his life, and that he wanted her for a wife. But he had just one hesitation. *I want to be sure that she can accept my mother, and even be willing to go to my village to preach to my people someday. And I want to know how my mother feels about her.*

When he spoke to Alfonso about the proposed trip, the response was more than positive. "That would be a thrill for us, Salvador. After hearing your story and all that happened to your family and the people in that village, I had hoped that I could go there. I am sure that my wife will feel the same."

It wasn't long before Salvador arranged to take Mayra and her parents on the long trip to his village to meet his mother and sisters. Later he told me on the phone that the acceptance was mutual. "Myra loves my mother, and my mother loves her and wants her for a daughter-in-law."

The last question had been settled. Although he had felt God's hand in finding Mayra for him, he wanted to be sure that she really was God's choice. As he kept thinking it over, one thought kept coming to his mind. *I have prayed for the right wife. After all that has happened in my life, I am convinced that God has been leading me. I feel called to the ministry, and I know it is important to marry someone who shares my goals. But I had no idea that God would bring the girl who could so completely capture my heart too. How I love her! This has to be a miracle!*

Salvador had described his childhood home and village so vividly that it had no real surprises for Mayra. But when she met his mother, she was filled with a feeling that she could hardly define, even to herself. She recognized in the humble little woman the kind of strength of character that enabled her to survive the tragedies in her life and still keep her faith in God. In Magdalena's eyes she saw the pain that Salvador's mother had suffered and the deep love for her son, who had been lost and then found. Even though she was living with the barest necessities of life, peace and acceptance filled her soul. *I already love this woman,* Mayra thought to herself. *She and I will be friends. We both love the same man, though in different ways.*

Once alone with her, Salvador asked the question that would determine their future, "Mayra, I asked God to bring me the right wife, the one He has chosen for me. I had no idea that He could find one so perfect for me as you. I was interested in qualifications, but God knew I needed a wife that I could love with all my heart. You are that one. You said that you would marry a minister.

Now, I want to know, would you be willing to marry this minister?"

She looked at him with her heart in her eyes and said, "Yes, Salvador, I would love to marry this minister!"

He took her in his arms and tenderly kissed her. "My dearest Mayra, I will love you and care for you as long as I live." True to the consecrated minister that he was, he added, "God has brought you to me. Let's pray together, to dedicate our lives to Him, and to ask for His blessing on our future together." Tears filled their eyes as they rose from their knees. Their happiness was compounded by the assurance that heaven approved of their love.

Salvador's district was in the hills and his churches scattered. He had no transportation except the local busses, and many times they didn't go where he needed to. Frequently he ended up walking for miles carrying his equipment.

At first Ken and I thought of trying to get him a motorcycle. However, considering the downpours Guatemala has during the rainy season, that didn't seem practical. After talking to some of our ICC supporters, I began to raise money for transportation for Salvador. Then I called him to see how much a good used Toyota pickup would cost him. He did find a good bargain. However I lacked a little of the price until Mary Lou Ham, who had taken the trip with us to his village, phoned and said, "I am sending $3,500 to help Salvador. Actually, it is the money I got from selling the puppies from our little mother bulldog." It was more than the cost of the truck, but she suggested we give the rest to him for whatever he needed. He bought a projector for his meetings along with other equipment and some furniture for their new home. When I learned that Salvador had baptized approximately 300 people that first year, I knew that he would put that vehicle to good use.

Finally the phone call came that I expected. "Mommy Fleck, Mayra and I are planning to be married. We both want our wedding right there at The Pines in the Rancho.

"Also we want you to be there and we want Poppy Fleck to marry us! And we want Ron and Bobbie to come too. We want them to be our padrinos." In Latin American weddings a couple, who are close family or friends, stand up with the couple, one from the groom's family and one from the bride's. Ron and Bobbie, our son and daughter-in-law, had sponsored Salvador all the way through college, and the year before we had taken him to visit them and to give a presentation in their church.

"Well, Salvador, congratulations! But I can't say I'm surprised, and I was sure you would want your wedding at The Pines. How does Mayra feel about that?"

"You know, I guess she knows how much I love The Pines. It is almost her idea! We are deciding on a date, but we want to be sure when you can come."

"I'll have to talk to Poppy Fleck and Ron and then let you know. By the way, do you think your mother will be able to come?" I was sure that she had never been out of her mountains before.

"Oh, yes, my mother will be there. In fact, I'll go and get her."

The date was finally agreed on when we could all get away. It would be a momentous trip. Besides the thrill of attending the wedding, it was the first time Ron had returned to the place he had grown up as a missionary kid.

Thus he and his wife, Bobbie, for the first time, saw ICC in action. We all stayed at the city center with the babies and then with the children at The Pines. Since Ron speaks Spanish, he could relate to the children, and he had a crowd of little boys following him all over the place.

Then we followed the same precautions as the year before. Juana arranged to have several cars escort us through the jungle. Among them was Salvador with his red pickup.

When we met Mayra for the first time I could readily see why he had chosen her. Many members of her family had arrived for the wedding, and Salvador's mother and two of his sisters came in their colorful typical dresses. His stepfather was there too. It would be a big occasion. The children at The Pines all helped to decorate the Rancho with palm branches and greenery gathered from the nearby forest and jungle. Pine needles covered the floor. Everything was beautiful. The housemothers and Juana all helped prepare the food for the reception. Everyone was happy to assist with the wedding.

Salvador wanted both of his mothers to walk up the aisle with him. I was on one side, and his little Indian mother on the other. Mayra was beautiful in her white wedding gown, and Salvador was a handsome groom.

As Ken stood there performing the ceremony, I

thought about the day, years before, when he had baptized Salvador down in the river. "When I came up out of the water," the boy told me later, "it seemed as if all the grief, pain, and anger rolled off my shoulders and I was a new person." It was a miracle how God had brought this child to us. Now Salvador is a minister with a wife whom God had saved especially for him.

And then my mind went back still farther—to the day I was struggling with the decision out in the woods in my private sanctuary and I realized that my problem was a fear of failure. I remembered the quotation: "But when we give ourselves wholly to God, and in our work follow His directions, He makes Himself responsible for its accomplishment. He would not have us conjecture as to the success of our honest endeavors. Not once should we think of failure." Today ICC cares for more than 1,200 children around the world in 16 countries. God has blessed our humble efforts beyond what we could ask or think.

Standing there at Salvador's wedding, I thought of God's protection that had continually surrounded us and how God had spoken to me, "Why are you so afraid? Don't you know you have a Father who loves you?" How many times He had proved that love for us.

Sitting there in that Rancho full of children, with those beautiful young people on the rostrum saying their vows, and thinking of all of the rest of our ICC family, I could humbly and earnestly pray, "Thank You so much for pushing me to take that leap of faith!"

Epilogue

What will happen to International Children's Care when you and Ken retire?" people often ask us. So many ministries disappear when the original founders, with their vision and dedication, are no longer involved. This is a question that needed to be addressed. It especially concerned us in the earlier years when Ken and I, both volunteers, were carrying most of the load. We wanted to build a solid foundation and ensure the future of this program for children. During the 22 years we spent with ICC we saw the fledgling orphan program grow into a strong organization with dedicated and professional staff. Witnessing many of our older children go on to higher education and finding their places in life has particularly thrilled us. Some of them are joining the ICC program and assuming responsibility.

With ICC in 16 countries and still growing, the demands on our time and energies continued to increase. We began to think seriously of what we should be doing to ensure the future for our children, while taking lesser responsibility ourselves. The ICC board, composed of professional and business people with many skills, has supported the development of wise and careful plans for the future, and the program is going strong, even though Ken and I are not as involved as before.

Our son, Rick, is currently president, and his wife, Sharon, has taken over my responsibilities as director of children's services. They have been involved with ICC for many years, inheriting not only our roles as leaders, but also our love and dedication to the children. Ken and I are still members of the board, and as founders and senior advisors, are still active in the program.

As I wrote the last chapters of this book, I took a computer along with me to Desert Hot Springs, where we were spending a few weeks. While Ken climbed the mountains around there, I spread my equipment out in the motor home and lost myself to the surroundings.

While there we attended the Palm Springs church. One Sabbath they dedicated the service to Walla Walla College alumni. At the potluck following the service we found ourselves at a table with Dr. and Mrs. Louis Smith. I was delighted. For some time I had wanted to thank him for his part in possibly saving my life. He remembered me and my former health problem. "I won't ever forget that morning in surgery," he told me. "Everything was ready, the surgery crew was waiting for you, but I asked for more time. Looking at the picture on the board, I couldn't bring myself to go through with it. I felt there were too many risks for you even though I was under a lot of pressure from everyone else to go ahead."

Then I reminded Dr. Smith of the visit five years later when I was on my way to Guatemala. "Yes, I remember," he said. "When I heard about your plans, I knew they would be successful! I'm not surprised at what God has done with ICC for the children of the world."

The next day I went back to my computer to finish this story with renewed confidence in God's promises. Reviewing those years, I could see so clearly how only God could have orchestrated events to make this program for children what it is today.